THE ART
of
WAR

The Weapons of Our Warfare

by:

Dr. Gene Herndon

© 2018 Gene Herndon. All Rights Reserved. Unauthorized Duplication is Prohibited.

Copyright © 2018 Gene Herndon. United States of America. All Rights Reserved under international copyright laws. Contents and/or cover may not be reproduced in whole or in part without prior written consent.

Printed in the United States of America

Published by Aion Multimedia
20118 N 67th Ave
Suite 300-446
Glendale AZ 85308
www.aionmultimedia.com

ISBN-13: 978-1-7330332-0-6

Scripture quotations unless otherwise noted are taken from the King James Bible, New York: American Bible Society: 1999.

Contents

PRINCIPLE 1: THE ART of STRATAGEMS 1
HE WHO KNOWS HIS ENEMY AND HIMSELF NEED NOT FEAR THE RESULT OF A HUNDRED BATTLES.

PRINCIPLE 2: THE ART of PREPARATION 21
RELY NOT ON THE LIKELYHOOD OF YOUR ENEMY NOT COMING TO ATTACK, BUT ON YOUR READINESS TO RECEIVE HIM.

PRINCIPLE 3: THE ART of FAITH 35
THY ENEMY'S WARFARE IS ALWAYS BASED ON DECEPTION.

PRINCIPLE 4: THE ART of AUTHORITY 47
VICTORIOUS WARRIORS WIN FIRST, AND THEN GO TO WAR.

PRINCIPLE 5: THE ART of COURAGE 59
IF THY WILL FACE THY FEAR, EVEN UNTO DEATH, THERE IS NOTHING THOU WILL NOT ACHIEVE.

PRINCIPLE 6: THE ART of COUNTERBALANCE STRATEGY 69
YOUR ENEMY'S GREATEST ATTACKS COME IN THE SEASONS THAT ARE MOST ADVANTAGEOUS TO HIM.

PRINCIPLE 7: THE ART of CORRESPONDING ACTION 79
FAITH WITHOUT ACTION IS THE SLOWEST ROUTE TO VICTORY. ACTION WITHOUT FAITH IS THE NOISE BEFORE DEFEAT.

PRINCIPLE 8: THE ART of LAYING PLANS 91
HAVING THE RIGHT PLAN LEADS TO VICTORY. BRUTE STRENGTH IS NOT ENOUGH..

PRINCIPLE 9: THE ART of UNITY 105
A WINNING ARMY MUST BE UNITED BY THE SAME SPIRIT THROUGHOUT ALL ITS RANKS.

INTRODUCTION

This book comes from a sermon series I preached based around ideas from an ancient book called *The Art of War*, written by Sun Tzu. It has been used in business as well as in modern-day warfare. It is a treatise that helps people understand how to go to war. It was written in ancient times, and it's still being used today.

Secular ideas are often rooted in biblical ideology, biblical understanding, and biblical doctrine. Some people pay a whole bunch of money to learn stuff they'd figure out if they just studied their Bible.

God's got all the answers. He really does, and there's nothing new under the sun.

We need to have a biblical worldview. There is a battle raging whether you know it or not, whether you wish to participate in it or not! There is a battle going on. So what I am endeavoring to do within the course of this book is give you some principles you can apply in your life, some practical wisdom to give you a greater understanding and greater skill on how to win the battles that come into your life.

THE ART OF WAR

Principle 1

THE ART *of* STRATAGEMS

HE WHO KNOWS HIS ENEMY AND HIMSELF NEED NOT FEAR THE RESULT OF A HUNDRED BATTLES.

When you don't know your enemy and don't know yourself, you will fail every time! Most people who have such high levels of fear regarding spiritual things don't understand this. We have to invest our time into beginning to understand who our enemy is—and I want you to be clear about my purpose and intent; it is not to glorify Satan in any way, shape, or form, but it *is* to expose his strategy.

"The Art of Stratagems" will help you understand that there are keys, there are ways, there are things that you need to do, strategies that you need to employ in order for you to be successful and walk in the victory that God has already purchased for believers in Christ.

Too many Christians are waiting for the moment when they arrive in heaven because they think that's where their victory is. But you can have heaven on Earth! And that doesn't mean that life will be without problems, because many are the afflictions of the righteous, but the Bible says God delivers us out of them all.

So we have to know our enemy, we have to understand his strategies, and then we have to know who *we* are, how we fit, the authority we've been given, and the way we are supposed to live in order to operate in that victory. Once you know your enemy and yourself, you need not fear the result of a hundred battles! It doesn't matter how many battles come into your life or how many trials come at you—it just doesn't matter, because you know you've got the victory!

> **Mark 5:1-10**
> And they came over unto the other side of the sea, into the country of the Gadarenes. And when he was come out of the ship, immediately there met him out of the tombs a man with an unclean spirit, who had his dwelling among the tombs; and no man could bind him, no, not with chains: because that he had been often bound with fetters and chains, and the chains had been plucked asunder by him, and the fetters broken in pieces: neither could any man tame him. And always, night and day, he was in the mountains, and in the tombs, crying, and cutting himself with stones. But when he saw Jesus afar off, he ran and worshipped him, and cried with a loud voice, and said, What have I to do with thee, Jesus, thou Son of the most high God? I adjure thee by God, that thou torment me not. For he said unto him, Come out of the man, thou unclean spirit. And he asked him, What is thy name? And he answered, saying, My name is Legion: for we are many. And he besought him much that he would not send them away out of the country.

I want you to see a few things happening here. You need to understand there are two worlds in operation at all times. Whether you like it or not, whether you are aware of it or not, an evil supernatural force is functioning and operating in our universe.

Here comes this man; he meets Jesus, and verse 2 says he had an unclean spirit and was running around in a cemetery! He was often bound in fetters and chains, he was *literally* busting out of chains! An unclean spirit inside him had the ability to infuse him with the supernatural strength to *bust chains*.

Did you know that the highest grossing movie genre of all time is horror movies? It's interesting how the media and the world give so much credit to what Satan can do without ever recognizing that Satan is a being created by our God. Whatever Satan can do, God can always do more and better!

Why do we spend so much time giving Satan glory for what little bit of power he has?

More importantly, if Satan was able to empower this man to break chains, then why do Christians act so wimpy? Why are we portrayed as so weak?

Let's be clear. On August 8, 2018, Fox News story described a radical Islamist who was arrested at a filthy New Mexico compound where he was reportedly training 11 malnourished children to commit school shootings with an assault rifle. If this man had been a Christian, the story would have been *all over the news*. Why are people so afraid to call out radical Islam? Because they're radical! And no one wants to be the next target! Now, I don't advocate violence. I want you to understand my point: A lot of things are demonic, and you don't even know it because the world is geared a certain way. But listen—we have power!

The demonized man in our scripture was running around night and day; he couldn't sit still. You could probably say he had ADHD! Think about it! And did you notice what else he was doing? He was *crying*. Spiritual torments can affect people's emotions in ways that can cause them to become emotionally unstable.

Not only that, it says he was cutting himself—and it was because of the spirit that was attacking him, causing him to want to inflict bodily harm on himself, maybe eventually kill himself.

When he saw Jesus, the man ran to him—but the *spirit* spoke. The spirit knew who Jesus was! That man had never met Jesus. All he knew was that something told him to run over and bow down!

How did he know that it was Jesus, Son of the Most High God?

How did he know that Jesus had the ability to deal with him?

Jesus was conversing with a person who was completely yielded to Satan! So His conversation was really not with the *man*, but with a spirit made up of thousands of spirits!

This is why the Bible says we wrestle not with flesh and blood, but against principalities and powers.

You can't run around thinking that everything you go through is a natural thing.

Some people hate you just because you are a believer. Some people hate you because they hate the Christ in you. I'm sure you've had some conversations where maybe you were wondering "What in the *world*? Why do they have such an issue with me? Why are they attacking me on Facebook?" It's because Christ in you, the hope of glory, is stirring stuff up and getting you to a place beyond their scope, and they are mad! They're trying to figure out, "How do I bring you into *my* world so that I can bait you into a fight?"

Never forget this: If Satan cannot fight you directly, he will bait you into one. And God forbid if you're in one that ain't yours, trying to save everybody else! That's a whole different message.

Getting back to Mark 5, where is this "Legion"? Where are these thousands and thousands and thousands of devils? Where do they reside?

They're in the man.

Their request wasn't "Don't throw us out of this man." Their request was *"Don't throw us out of this area."* Why? Because they want *territory.*

This is why you can go to certain places in the world, certain states, certain cities, and you will see certain things that you won't see in other places. There are territories! You hop off the plane in Las Vegas (when it lands, obviously)—and some people get stupid! You can *sense* that the atmosphere has changed.

Legion didn't care about the man anymore—and remember, there were *thousands* of demons in this *one man*, which should help you understand that you're a lot bigger on the inside than you think you are!

They weren't even fighting as to who was going to talk! None of them said to the speaking demon, *"Hey!* You got to speak last time, I wanna talk this time!" When you deal with things of demonic and satanic nature, you need to know they are not fighting among themselves. They understand rank; they understand authority; they're not criticizing one another; they know exactly what they're there to do—to wreak havoc! They've got the same purpose, and the same mind.

If you want to find dysfunction, you've got to come to the church! If you want to find people who complain and talk bad about the pastor, the

Jesus was saying, "If the miracles I did in your city, in your territory, in your region had been done in these horrible cities, they would have repented and changed their lives!"

The people of Bethsaida had become so desensitized to the moving of God's Spirit that they couldn't see all the miracles He was doing right in the midst of their town. How in the world did they get to the place where He said, "If I had done for those bad guys what I did for you, they would have repented a long time ago"?

Take a look at what Jesus did right in front of these people.

> **Mark 8:22-26**
> **And he cometh to Bethsaida; and they bring a blind man unto him, and besought him to touch him. And he took the blind man by the hand, and led him out of the town; and when he had spit on his eyes, and put his hands upon him, he asked him if he saw ought. And he looked up, and said, I see men as trees, walking. After that he put his hands again upon his eyes, and made him look up: and he was restored, and saw every man clearly. And he sent him away to his house, saying, Neither go into the town, nor tell it to any in the town.**

Do you see why He told them not to go back there? (

He said "That area, it's not that they're evil—they're *apathetic*. They don't even care. Even evil people, when they see good, can change. But these folks over here?"

This is the only place in the Bible where you see Jesus laying hands on someone twice. Every other time, when Jesus laid hands on somebody, they got healed the first time! What I want you to understand is this: You can have eyesight ... and no *insight*. The problem He was dealing with was not the fact that this man couldn't see—that was just one of the problems. The second problem was that he couldn't process what he *did* see. Jesus laid hands on him and asked, "What do you see?" The man said, "I see men as trees, walking."

How do you explain what things look like to someone who has never seen before? Especially when, all of a sudden, they can see! He used his best explanation of what he thought it was— "Men as trees, walking." That's what he thought it was.

Jesus laid hands on him a second time and said "Now, what I need you to have is not only eyesight, but *insight*. You come out of a town that has eyesight, but they have no insight into what's happening, no ability to discern what's really going on. They are sitting, blithely unaware, in a world where things are happening all around them—and they have no idea what's going on! So now that I've given you eyesight, you're like them. But I need you to go one step further and have insight, too. Then when you see certain things, you can discern what they are the moment you see them. I don't want you to be so fleshly in your thinking that you don't realize you are in the middle of a battle in what seems harmless to you."

This is the problem when you have eyesight, but no insight. There is no question in my mind that you can see different things that are happening. You watch the news. You've got to be blind and deaf and dumb not to see what's happening in this world. *Clearly* something's not right. You are in the middle of a battle, and I hope that you are staying awake.

You can't just have eyesight—you've got to have insight.

I'll give you an example.

I thank God for our church building and I'm grateful for it. But I'm believing God for a new building somewhere out there for us to continue to grow into and be able to provide all of the programs and things we want to do for our kids. Years ago, in our old building, back before we had this one, I didn't really have an office. So I used to meet people at my "International Headquarters"—which was a coffee shop. I have, like, 5,000 of them all around the world!

When I would meet someone at a coffee shop for a counseling session— let's say they happened to be a female—I would always pray, "Lord, don't let this person start crying!" Because here we are, in the coffee shop, this big black guy and this poor little woman, she's over there crying, and you can see people sipping on their coffee looking at me like I'm a *Big Old Meanie*. I'm over here trying to help! I'm bringing the Word of God, I'm bringing godly counsel, I'm doing the God thing!

Eyesight ... no insight.

When you know your enemy and you know yourself, you need not fear the result of a hundred battles, because you will see it. It'll be crystal clear for you. That's why when Jesus got the man all sorted out to where he could see and interpret what he saw, he said, "Now, don't go back there!"

I see this with Christians. They get into the church; they start doing well; God starts moving for them; they start getting better; and then all of a sudden, the pull of the world drags them down. God set them free and delivered them from liquor, drugs, etc., and then all of a sudden, they want to go back! And once they start going back, all of the light and insight they used to have is gone! This is why the Bible says a righteous man falls seven times, but he gets back up. You've got to get back up! It matters who you hang around, who your friends are, the people who surround you, what people in your family you allow. It matters what world you live in. It matters!

Jesus said, "Now that I've got you set free, now that I've got you seeing properly, don't you dare go back to what you came out of!"

"Well, I'm going back to minister to them," you say. No you're not! You ain't been around long enough!

It's funny how people who struggle with alcohol talk about "going to the bar to minister to a friend." No, you're not! Once you get in that bar, they're going to start ministering to *you*!

Listen, it's very simple; if you know your enemy, then your enemy knows you too!

And if he knows you?

Putting a drink in front of me doesn't do much, but chocolate cake is a whole different problem! I can walk into a bar and walk out—but let me walk into a bakery!

Here's what we're going to have to do, let me make you a deal. You let me go into the bar and minister to people, and I'll send you to the bakery to minister to folks. I know I'll mess around in the bakery and eat everything on the menu except for "Please," "Thank you," and "Come Again"!

If your enemy knows you, and you don't know yourself? This is how you get yourself into situations you should not be in.

God has a plan for how relationships are supposed to function—here you are, a good Christian girlfriend, over at his house, Netflix and chillin', and then wondering why the next morning you have regrets. You shouldn't have been there in the first place!

You say, "Well, we should be able to hang out and just watch a movie and let that be that." Well, no.

Go watch a movie in a movie theater with a hundred other people. People who are actually watching.

It's easier to avoid than it is to resist, and if Satan knows what your weakness is?

I have seen many a woman and many a man pull many a man and many a woman out of their church. It is very, very common. I mean it's one of those things where you can almost count the *days*.

"Oh, my God! They got hooked up with *who*?"

It's just a matter of time, because Satan knows your weakness. He knows how lonely you're going to get. It hits you at that moment when you are the loneliest. You get on the phone at still-dark-o'clock in the morning like "Oh, I just need somebody to hang out with." No, you don't! Get your narrow behind back to sleep! Ain't much open past midnight but legs!

> **Acts 16:16-18**
> **And it came to pass, as we went to prayer, a certain damsel possessed with a spirit of divination met us, which brought her masters much gain by soothsaying: The same followed Paul and us, and cried, saying, These men are the servants of the most high God, which shew unto us the way of salvation.**

THE ART OF STRATAGEMS

And this did she many days. But Paul, being grieved, turned and said to the spirit, I command thee in the name of Jesus Christ to come out of her. And he came out the same hour.

To whom is Paul talking here? *The spirit.*

Who's in front of him? *The girl.*

She was possessed with a spirit of divination, and she brought her masters much gain by soothsaying.

Do you know what soothsaying is? Crystal balls, fortune-telling, reading palms, your horoscope—and if you're into that kind of thing, stop. You have no idea what it is you're playing with. It is not godly in any way, shape, or form.

She was *possessed*.

The Greek word for *possessed* is rooted in the word from which we get "echo." *Echo* is when you stand over a cavern and shout "Hello!" and you hear "Hello! ... Hello! ..." Right?

One of the definitions for *echo* is "one who slavishly repeats the words and opinions of another."

The girl in our passage *echoed* a spirit of divination. So everything she said was an echo of what the spirit of divination said. And by that, she earned her masters money because the spirit of divination can see into the realm of the spirits and tell you things!

This is like those TV shows with mediums who say things like "Your grandmother came through, and she told me she buried her prize ring in the northwest corner of your property. So if you go dig over there by that fencepost, you'll find it."

And the person goes home and digs by the fencepost, finds it, and says, "Oh, my God! My grandmother is talking to me!" Your grandmother's not talking to you. What's talking to you is the familiar spirit that has been following your family, the spirit that sat there and watched your grandmother bury that ring in that spot! *That* spirit is speaking, and it needs someone to echo them.

> **Acts 16:17-18**
> **The same followed Paul and us, and cried, saying, These men are the servants of the most high God, which shew unto us the way of salvation. And this she did many days. But Paul, being grieved, turned and said to the spirit, I command thee in the name of Jesus Christ to come out of her. And he came out the same hour.**

How did she know Paul was a servant of the Most High God?

She *didn't* know. She was echoing. The *spirit* knew.

The spirit was thinking, "Those are some Jesus folks right there—do they see us? Do they have eyesight *and* insight? Little girl, go over there and just say something to them, let's see if he *really* sees us. Tell him he's a servant of the Most High God, play to his ego and let's see what happens. I just need to know if he sees us! Because if he doesn't see us, we can keep operating and making money! But if he sees us? I don't want him sneaking up on me unaware! So go play with him, go mess with him. Go say stuff to him."

Now watch this—she did this for *many days*.

So that means Day 1: She starts talking to Paul; he doesn't say a word.

Day 2: He doesn't say anything.

Day 3: However many days this goes on, I don't know. More of the same.

"Several" is seven, so let's just say "many" is eight. We could say it's five, it doesn't really matter. The question becomes "Why does Paul act on the fifth-or-so day?"

It says that Paul was *grieved*. The Greek word for *grieved* means something agitated his spirit. He finally turned and said to her, "Spirit! I command thee in the name of Jesus, come out of her!" And it came out right at that moment!

Here's the point I want you to see: At least four days passed before Paul had the agitation in his spirit to do it. Then all of a sudden God quickened his spirit, and he became agitated and he *knew*. God told him to deal with it.

Here is the problem in the Body of Christ: People think they see something; they have eyesight. They might even have a *little bit* of insight, but they do not have a leading to deal with the issue. So they're laying hands on people, wondering why people aren't getting delivered.

Just because you *know* something is demonic doesn't mean that God told *you* to deal with it! Some things are to keep you aware and informed of what's going on around you. Skill will help you to know when the agitation is there, and *that's* when it's time. Stop trying to punch people in the nose, and start dealing with the Spirit working in you!

Paul didn't pop the girl in the head and say, "Girl, stop following me!"

It took him four or five days, *at least*, before he finally had an agitation in his spirit, and then he said, "OK, *now* it's time to deal with this."

He could have backhanded her, kept his pimp hand strong! Think about it!

I need you to understand because so many fleshly people want to get into their flesh and start swingin', thinking, "This is how I'm-a deal with you, this is how I'm-a deal with this. You done got on my *last* nerve; you've done this one too many times!"—never realizing that is *not* the way God fights.

This is what got them (the disciples) thrown in prison; it wasn't because they got the girl delivered, but because they were *messing up her masters' money*.

It's funny that Christians get upset when a preacher tells them God *wants* them to have money—but then they go and work 40, 50, 60 hours a week to get it. They get ruffled if a preacher says God wants you to be blessed. It's not for *you*, but to be a blessing! There's a purpose behind it!

Here these guys in our scripture were *literally* pimping out this girl—not sexually, but they were using her for her "gift" (more of a curse, actually) that echoed the spirit realm and made them all kinds of money. She wasn't even making the money! She was a victim of a process! The moment she got delivered and was in her right mind, they were mad! They brought Paul in front of the council to put him in jail because he was messing up their money.

Satan wants Christians to be poor and not to experience the prosperity God desires for His people. When you begin experiencing things beyond your natural limitations, you've ventured into Satan's territory and are messing with his money! He wants to direct the wealth of the wicked as he desires and won't willingly allow any Christian to challenge his plan.

If you're a believer and you have the Holy Ghost working inside you, you also are able to echo what God says. This is why no matter where Joseph ended up—he was in the pit, he was in prison, he was in the palace—but no matter where Joseph went, he prospered. Why? Because he had the Holy Ghost working! He was God's man! Now, the Holy Ghost was not *inside* him because he lived under the Old Testament, but the Holy Ghost was working *on* him. Therefore, everywhere he went, he prospered.

The company you work for prospers because *you are there*. Why do you let them make money off of your gift and drive around in fancy cars and fly around in fancy jets?

Why do people go to soothsayers looking for their fortunes and horoscopes?

Because they want answers.

The question is: Would you like *an* answer, or would you like *the* answer?

If you want *the* answer, the Bible says the Holy Ghost is inside you and will teach you all things.

> **Luke 4:38-41**
> **And he arose out of the synagogue, and entered into Simon's house. And Simon's wife's mother was taken with a great fever; and they besought him for her. And he stood over her, and rebuked the fever; and it left her: and immediately she arose and ministered unto them. Now when the sun was setting, all they that had any sick with divers diseases**

> brought them unto him; and he laid his hands on every one of them, and healed them. And devils also came out of many, crying out, and saying, Thou art Christ the Son of God. And he rebuking them suffered them not to speak: for they knew that he was Christ.

Simon's mother-in-law was struck with a fever. Many theologians believe this was some kind of epileptic seizure. Jesus rebuked it, and she got up and literally started serving them, cooking for them, and waiting on them. Right?

When spirits started coming out of sick people later on, they knew *exactly* who Jesus was—that was *insight*. Insight with no eyesight. And Jesus shut them down. He was like, "Shut up! Don't say another word, because if you know who I am, then *you know I AM WHO I AM.*"

The phrase "Taken with a great fever"—do you know what that is?

That's an echo. That saying is the *same word* as the Greek "echo."

In other words, she didn't have a fever!

The spirit *affecting* her had a fever! It was producing a certain characteristic or trait in her, and it was echoing it. This is why she grew no better until someone was able to see beyond *eyesight* and look with *insight*. This is why Jesus said, "This kind only comes out but with prayer and fasting" (Mark 9:29).

Prayer and fasting do not create more power in you! You can pray and not eat for the rest of your life, and you will not be any more powerful than you are today. What prayer-and-fasting does is give you greater visual acuity; it gives you a greater ability to understand *insight* so you can see *into* a situation and discern what it is, so then you can respond accordingly and deal with it.

It is intelligence! It's intel! The Holy Ghost is inside us. We're supposed to be echoing Him so that when a demonic thing pops up with a problem, the Holy Ghost pops up with an answer!

The phrase "was taken" comes from two words that mean "together" and "to hold."—in other words, "to hold together." It's likened in some ways to wearing a garment, like putting on a jacket or a sweater. If you are a spirit, you live in a body and you possess a soul. So, "to take hold of" and "wear like a garment" means that the body of someone possessed by a demon has been put on like a garment by a demon. If I take off my suit jacket, lay it on the ground, and it starts moving? Something's wrong! But as long as it's on *me*, when I'm moving, it moves.

Whatever Simon's mother-in-law was experiencing was because she was moved as the demon moved. As it responded, so did she. As it experienced fever, she had a fever. When Jesus spoke to the deaf and dumb boy saying, "Come out", if the boy was *actually* deaf and dumb, how did he hear Jesus say "Come out"?

The point is if demonic spirits are seeking a means to "echo" their wants, then how can you know if someone is yielded to them? If you see only with your eyesight but not insight, you might pinch them and they move. You say, "Oh, they're alive!" But *what's moving?*

In the spiritual realm, possession, depression, and oppression are all different manifestations of demonic activity.

If you are a believer with the Holy Ghost residing inside you, you cannot be *possessed*. To be "possessed" means that a person's body is completely taken over by a demon that has put them on like a garment and has started running things.

But believers can be *oppressed* and *depressed*. And you have to know the difference. You have to know what's affecting you, because spiritual warfare is real.

> **Ezekiel 28:1-7**
> **The word of the LORD came again unto me, saying, Son of man, say unto the prince of Tyrus, Thus saith the Lord GOD; Because thine heart is lifted up, and thou hast said, I am a God, I sit in the seat of God, in the midst of the seas; yet thou art a man, and not God, though thou set thine heart as the heart of God: Behold, thou art wiser than Daniel; there is no secret that they can hide from thee: With thy wisdom and**

> with thine understanding thou hast gotten thee riches, and hast gotten gold and silver into thy treasures: By thy great wisdom and by thy traffick hast thou increased thy riches, and thine heart is lifted up because of thy riches: Therefore thus saith the Lord GOD; Because thou hast set thine heart as the heart of God; Behold, therefore I will bring strangers upon thee, the terrible of the nations: and they shall draw their swords against the beauty of thy wisdom, and they shall defile thy brightness.

In this verse, the prophet is speaking to a person, a prince who is a very rich and successful ruler and businessperson. And he says, "You have done a lot of things that have gotten you to a place of success, but none of it was My doing. And now you're starting to believe your own press because you are wealthy!"

> **Ezekiel 28:12-13**
> Son of man, take up a lamentation upon the king of Tyrus, and say unto him, Thus saith the Lord GOD; Thou sealest up the sum, full of wisdom, and perfect in beauty. Thou hast been in Eden the garden of God; every precious stone was thy covering, the sardius, topaz, and the diamond, the beryl, the onyx, and the jasper, the sapphire, the emerald, and the carbuncle, and gold: the workmanship of thy tabrets and of thy pipes was prepared in thee in the day that thou wast created."

The prophet tells this ruler, "You're nothing but a man."

In verse 12, God tells Ezekiel, "Speak to the king. What I want you to do is prophesy to the king that's running this ruler—you have been in Eden, the garden of God."

Best I know, there were only three people in Eden, and Adam and Eve are super dead! They've been that way a long time, right? So *who in the world* is God talking to?

Because there's only one person left!

> **Ezekiel 28:20-22**

> **Again the word of the LORD came unto me, saying, Son of man, set thy face against Zidon, and prophesy against it, And say, Thus saith the Lord GOD; Behold, I am against thee, O Zidon; and I will be glorified in the midst of thee: and they shall know that I am the LORD, when I shall have executed judgments in her, and shall be sanctified in her.**

The prophet spoke to the man, the prince, the businessman, the ruler in charge—Eyesight!

Now he speaks to *Satan*—Insight!

He says that Satan was the king leading this prince (and presidents and rulers and business people) who have all become highly successful and made all kinds of money. Satan leads this whole system.

Lastly, he says "Let me talk to this city, this territory. I'm-a get that thorn off of you. They've despised you, they've hated you, they've been attacking you, I'm going to lay 'em down low."

That's a thorn. A thorn is an attack—not a sickness.

It's called The Law of First Mention. After things are first mentioned biblically, that's their meaning throughout scripture. I've heard people say that Paul's thorn was sickness. No, it was not. It was absolutely what he said it was—a messenger sent from Satan to harass him.

God told Ezekiel to speak to the man, speak to what's controlling the man, and speak to the city or territory the man was in.

Here you thought you elected presidents and kings, that you had something to do with it—standing in that booth with your little pen, wearing your "I voted today!" sticker. Now, I'm not telling you not to vote, because you should! That's exercising your right, and you need to. If you don't, then don't complain about how it turned out! But you also need more than eyesight. Have insight.

> **Revelation 13:1-5**
> **And I stood upon the sand of the sea, and saw a beast rise up out of the sea, having seven heads and ten horns, and upon his horns ten crowns, and upon his heads the name of**

blasphemy. And the beast which I saw was like unto a leopard, and his feet were as the feet of a bear, and his mouth as the mouth of a lion: and the dragon gave him his power, and his seat, and great authority. And I saw one of his heads as it were wounded to death; and his deadly wound was healed: and all the world wondered after the beast. And they worshipped the dragon which gave power unto the beast: and they worshipped the beast, saying, Who is like unto the beast? who is able to make war with him? And there was given unto him a mouth speaking great things and blasphemies; and power was given unto him to continue forty and two months.

Here we have two players, two characters: We've got a beast, and we've got a dragon.

Who put in the work? *The beast.*

Who called the shots? *The dragon.*

Where did the beast get his power? *From the dragon.*

I'm going to help you: The dragon is Satan.

Our world is in the middle of a battle, and people don't even know it. They turn on the television and listen to what mainstream media says, they listen to all that's happening—they have eyesight, they can see it—but they don't stop to say "OK, God, give me some insight on this. Tell me what this really is. How do I nip this in the bud right now?"

He who understands his enemy and understands himself need not fear the result of a hundred battles! What is there to be afraid of when I know how the enemy works?

Some people are too "super spiritual." If their car doesn't start, they're like "Oh, this is the *devil*!" Um, no—you ain't had an oil change in fifty years! You're running with no oil in the car!

"It ain't nothin' but the *devil*!"

Their keyboard starts acting up "I rebuke you, devil!" No, change the batteries.

If an agitation rolls up in you and your spirit, then you'd better know that that's God talking to you, telling you that now is the time for you to deal with that. *That*'s the moment when you step up and say, "You know what, devil? I rebuke you! You have no right whatsoever. I rebuke you right now in the name of Jesus. You will not steal my joy, you will not steal my finances, you will not steal my health."

That spiritual agitation tells you that you are really in the midst of a battle.

Principle 2

THE ART *of* PREPARATION

RELY NOT ON THE LIKELIHOOD OF YOUR ENEMY NOT COMING TO ATTACK, BUT ON YOUR READINESS TO RECEIVE HIM.

Some people believe that their prayer life is enough to get Satan to leave them alone. They'll pray, "Just leave me alone, and you'll never be able to attack me again!"

Many are the afflictions of the righteous. We are not of this world, but we are *in* this world. As long as you are in this world, you will deal with an onslaught of attacks coming through a host of demonic forces that includes Satan himself. It is a challenge.

Sometimes I preach things I have experienced, and sometimes I experience things I have preached—no one is exempt! I don't care how spiritual a person thinks they are; no one is exempt from attack. And it's not that I've tried to find ways to try to keep his attacks from coming! I just focus my time on readiness to receive him when he comes.

> **Ephesians 6:10-13**
> **Finally, my brethren, be strong in the Lord, and in the power of his might. Put on the whole armour of God, that ye may be able to stand against the wiles of the devil. For we wrestle not against flesh and blood, but against principalities, against powers, against the rulers of the darkness of this world, against spiritual wickedness in high places. Wherefore take unto you the whole armour of God, that ye may be able to withstand in the evil day, and having done all, to stand.**

If you've never studied the Book of Ephesians, you should! The Book of Ephesians is considered to be the blueprint for Christian maturity. If you want to know how to grow up in your Christianity, if you want to learn how to walk in your Christianity, Ephesians is the book that will certainly help you do that!

There are three predominant concepts in the book of Ephesians, three prevailing themes: sit, walk, and stand. "Sit" is where you are, positionally, in Christ. "Walk" is how you live your life for Christ. "Stand" is how you resist sin and how you do warfare in Christ.

Ephesians has six chapters that cover these three general themes, and it helps you understand how to do battle in the realm of the spirit.

Many people ask, "Could you pray for me? Could you pray for God to give me direction and help me through these attacks?" Some of your challenges are your own creation, and no one can pray them away. You can't live in sin and then be upset by the consequences that come from it. God looks at how you live. God looks at the things you're doing.

More importantly: it isn't so much God punishing you as it is Satan seeking opportunity against you. And as Satan seeks opportunity against you, the things you find yourself caught up in can become the avenues by which he gains entrance into your life.

Paul wrote to the church at Ephesus, giving them teaching on things he wanted them to understand through this letter. When he wrote this letter, there were no Chapters 1 through 6. Those chapter divisions were added later in order to study Paul's letter and reference different portions of it. But when he wrote it, it was all just one big letter trying to help them understand, like "Dear Ephesians, These are things I want you to know. These are things I want you to discern. These are things I want to equip you with."

He told them to put on the full armor of God because they were wrestling not against flesh and blood, but against principalities and powers. Notice how this is a repetition of a theme from our preceding chapter where the prophet talked about dealing with people, with the prince, with the king

PRINCIPLE 2: THE ART OF PREPARATION

(or the ruler, so to speak), and with the demonic nature functioning in the world. Then he spoke to the land or the territories they control and in which they operate. The same principles of spiritual warfare apply in both scriptures, Old Testament and New. Part of our challenge as believers and as God's Church is recognizing that not everything is natural. You don't wrestle against flesh and blood.

A few times, I've walked into stores where salespeople were just *mean* to me, and I wondered, "Why? Why am I being treated like this? I watched this guy with other people; he was just nice as can be with them—smiling, all happy. Then they see me and start treating me like this."

There's a story of a Christian missionary who was overseas. He would go help in a particular village for a while. Then he'd leave and come back, leave and come back, again and again.

Finally, one of the leaders in the village said, "Could you possibly leave some people here to stay instead of coming and going?"

And the missionary said, "Why is that?"

"Every time, as soon as you leave, a group of shamans and witches come down out of the mountains and harass us! As soon as they spot you on your way back, they take off."

The missionary asked, "How do they know anything about us?"

They said, "They're afraid of you."

"Why?"

"They said you have a blood stain in the center of your forehead that they can't explain. They can see blood on you."

The blood wasn't there *physically*, but it was there in the realm of the spirit.

Demons recognize true believers. You are marked by God. Just because you have no understanding or discernment about who you are in Christ doesn't mean demons don't know who you are. If you are blithely unaware of spiritual forces in your life, you might experience stuff and wonder, "Why is this? What is it? What did I do wrong? What's wrong with me? What's going on?" You fail to realize you are marked by the blood of Jesus, and they can see it in the realm of the spirits. That means your very presence can agitate certain people!

This is why you might have had certain very good friends before you got saved, and *after* you got saved, they suddenly can't stand being around you. Why? *Because it's the Christ in you.* It's the hope of glory that agitates those devils.

When people are used to functioning in a demonic way, everything is OK. When y'all were backing it up into the club together, everything was OK. Everything was OK when you were throwing back drinks together. Everything was OK when he was watching football on Sunday instead of coming to church. Everything was wonderful until you made a stand and said, "I am going to live for God." The moment you made a decision toward God, you set yourself against a whole host of demonic beings and entities.

Satan is only one entity, and he can only be at one place at a time—he's not God! Therefore, you deal with a host of badly behaving demons. He doesn't deserve much of the credit we give him. We tend to think he is somehow more powerful than our omnipotent God. It's true that we wrestle not against flesh and blood, but against principalities and powers. So you don't need to punch people in the nose; you have what you need to give black eyes to Satan and his minions!

If you are a believer, you cannot have demons inside you. God will not share His presence with anyone else. Therefore, believers cannot be demon possessed. So demons have to apply *oppression* or get you into *depression*, which is all the same type of stuff, just pushing down on you to keep you subjected to their influence.

Imagine a boy and a girl who have been dating and have been intimate. Then they decide their relationship is not going to work, or one of them decides that and the other one can't let it go. Even worse, let's say one of them is being abused by the other, and she still can't let it go. I don't understand it. They're being *oppressed*, right?

PRINCIPLE 2: THE ART OF PREPARATION

This is where obsession comes in. You can become obsessed with someone because of the demonic nature of such mixed-up relationships.

So now you're like, "Girl, he beats you all day long!"

And she's like, "I know, but I could change him!" *Really?*

Let me put this out there: If *God* hasn't changed him, *you* are not going to change him. Can people change? Of course, they can. But you've got to realize that in some situations, you are dealing with demonic forces and not just that person!

Paul talks about two different worlds, and the beautiful thing about God is that He will allow you to conceptualize Him in whatever way you want to. You can't argue about my conception of God, because what I believe God to be is based not on what education I've matriculated into my life, but my experiences in my faith and my belief system concerning God. You may have a different belief system than me. You may have a different level of trust concerning God. Your concept of God may be different than mine. Yours could be bigger than mine, or yours could be smaller than mine. Our conceptions can be very different!

Truly, nothing you can say or do, nothing you can educate me with can begin to diminish what I believe God can do. If I am able to have my own conceptualization of who God is, then what business is it of a one-talent Christian to try to tell a five-talent Christian what God is able to do or not do? Whatever you function in, whatever your fears are, whatever your lack is, whatever your disbelief is, you cannot project that upon me and assume that I'm going to take on what you refuse to walk in. That means we can hold very different positions. God can be very real to me in a certain way, and His level of providing for me may be different than it is for you.

And if that is true, then God cannot be recognized; He can only be revealed. Recognition means you already have some specificity to say, to see, or to understand before you will believe in Him.

If it is true that God can do more than you could ask or think, then trust God. If God is capable of whatever level you can attain, then God can always go one step beyond you. How dare we not realize that there's way more at work in God than what our little brains can comprehend?

Many people want to develop in the things of God, but they don't want to *chase* God. They don't want to go after God. They don't want to seek Him first and His kingdom of righteousness—they want to seek their own selves, their own things, and they want to try to figure out "How can I make God deal with my revelation of Him?"

In truth, God will never fall to your level of revelation. But I can tell you this; your manifestation will never exceed your revelation.

Two different worlds operate around us. You can walk in one world and actually operate in another. You can be a victim of a world to which you pay no attention, while you wonder why things happen the way they do, why things don't seem to be the way you want them to be. All these different functions occur in the world, and you wonder where they come from.

> **2 Corinthians 12:1-2**
> **It is not expedient for me doubtless to glory. I will come to visions and revelations of the Lord. I knew a man in Christ above fourteen years ago, (whether in the body, I cannot tell; or whether out of the body, I cannot tell: God knoweth;) such an one caught up to the third heaven.**

In other words, "OK, listen; it's not helpful to brag, but let me tell you about some visions I've seen and things that have happened. I knew a guy (that is, myself) about 14 years ago who was caught up into the third heaven. The third heaven was paradise. I was in God's throne room. I heard things in that throne room that I cannot even tell you. I wish I could, but I can't! You ain't ready!" But listen, if you understand being caught up to a third heaven, then you understand that there's a second and a first heaven. The first heaven is the atmosphere; it's the sky where planes and birds fly around. The second heaven is the realm of demonic activity—and that's in Ephesians.

PRINCIPLE 2: THE ART OF PREPARATION

Ephesians 6:1
For we wrestle not against flesh and blood, but against principalities, against powers, against the rulers of the darkness of this world, against spiritual wickedness in high places.

When Jacob dreamt about that ladder, he saw angels ascending and descending, communicating, sending messages to and from the throne. Where were they going? They were going from the first heaven, through the second heaven, into the third heaven, and then bringing messages from the throne from the third heaven, through the second heaven, and into the first heaven.

Remember, in Daniel's vision, they were held up. They were fighting. They were warring. What were they warring against? Demonic spirits, demonic entities, spiritual wickedness in high places. The difference between their warfare and yours is that you have the Holy Ghost inside you. You have the hotline between you and God.

The Bible mentions three types of angels in the world. The first type are warring angels, of which Michael is the head. Next are the messenger angels, of which Gabriel is the head. Finally, are the worshipping angels—their head was *Satan*. He led worship for God.

This is why people on worship teams have to be careful, right? Because there is a pull or draw to forget that it is God working through you to lead others into worship, and begin focusing on yourself, which is *exactly* what caused Satan to fault—spiritual wickedness in high places.

Remember Jesus said, "I beheld Satan as lightning fall from heaven" (Luke 10:18).

Where did Satan fall from? The highest place, or, in other words, the third heaven. Satan doesn't have access to the throne room anymore. He can work only in the first and second heaven.

When Paul says, "Wherefore take unto you the whole armor of God," he's telling us that someone might be saved yet not be *saved*. Let's say you and I go to the mall, and we park right next to each other. It's raining, so I get out of my car, and I put up my umbrella. I watch you get out of your car, and you have an umbrella, but you don't put it up! So now you are soaking wet as we walk to the mall.

You turn to me and say, "I thought I wouldn't get wet because I'm saved!"

You *are*, but you refused to put up your umbrella!

This is what Paul means when he tells us to put on God's armor.

He's saying, "Yes, believer, you're saved—but you still have to put on the whole armor of God so that you may be able to withstand the battle against evil."

The prefix *anti* added to a word means "to withstand" or "to stand against." It's a military term. An antihistamine is an allergy medication that stands against the release of histamines into the body's bloodstream. It fights it back against the body's allergic response.

God has given you ways to fight spiritual battles. This chapter will help you understand what this armor is for and how to use it.

Paul wrote in Ephesians 6 to take the sword of the spirit, which is the Word of God. He also said to take the helmet of salvation, which is the substratum of all the rest. As the base on which we stand, the helmet of salvation is critically important.

> **Matthew 1:21**
> **And she shall bring forth a son, and thou shalt call his name Jesus: for he shall save his people from their sins**

We understand that *salvation* means "to be saved." So you know that if you are a believer in Christ, you are, in fact, saved. That word, *saved*, in its very essence, means that you have the life of God in you. To be *saved* means that you are removed from the death, from the doom, gloom, and destruction that was waiting for you. You are now translated into the kingdom of light. This is the traditional Christian understanding of salvation.

PRINCIPLE 2: THE ART OF PREPARATION

> **Matthew 14:29-30**
> And he said, Come. And when Peter was come down out of the ship, he walked on the water, to go to Jesus. But when he saw the wind boisterous, he was afraid; and beginning to sink, he cried, saying, Lord, SAVE me.

This is not the *traditional* sense of what we know salvation to be, but in Greek, it's the exact same word. Peter was calling to Jesus, "Save me," as in "Deliver me" or "Rescue me."

> **Jude 1:5**
> I will therefore put you in remembrance, though ye once knew this, how that the Lord, having SAVED the people out of the land of Egypt, afterward destroyed them that believed not.

Here the same word means "deliverance"—to *physically* deliver.

> **2 Timothy 4:18**
> And the Lord shall deliver me from every evil work, and will PRESERVE me unto his heavenly kingdom: to whom be glory for ever and ever. Amen.

That word, *preserve*, also refers to "safety" and means " keep me," "guard me."

It's the exact same Greek word as the one used to mean *salvation*.

> **Luke 8:36**
> They also which saw it told them by what means he that was possessed of the devils was HEALED.

Guess what? The word *healed* or *cured* is this same word that means "salvation." It means "to be rescued." It means "deliverance." It means "to be kept safe." It means "to be exorcised of demons."

> **Matthew 9:20-22**
> And, behold, a woman, which was diseased with an issue of blood twelve years, came behind him, and touched the hem

of his garment: For she said within herself, If I may but touch his garment, I shall be WHOLE. But Jesus turned him about, and when he saw her, he said, Daughter, be of good comfort; thy faith hath made thee WHOLE. And the woman was made WHOLE from that hour.

I know this seems like a Bible college lesson, but it is extremely important for you to see some of these things in order to progress to the next stage of understanding. One of the keys to this scripture eluded me for a while. Then one day I realized why this is so important and what exactly Paul is telling us to do.

One concept of salvation says, "If I believe in Jesus, I am now right with God and I can make it into heaven." That is a very basic, rudimentary understanding of what it is to be saved. But there's a whole list of things that occur in salvation:

- I have the right to be set free from all demonic oppression.
- I have the right in my physical body to be rescued when I'm in the midst of a bad situation.
- I have the right to be transferred into the kingdom of light, to function from that place and not have to suffer through this life.

Some things inherent in your salvation are not always clear. Most people think that in order to get delivered, they have to add something to salvation. That's one of my struggles with deliverance ministries.

Do I believe people need to get delivered? Yes, some people do.

But when someone develops an entire ministry to get people delivered and says they can break generational curses? Let me explain something to you. If Jesus hung on the cross for me, then He took all curses and nailed them to the cross. I don't need you to put your hands on me to get a generational curse out of my life; Jesus has already paid that price.

Therefore, I have the ability to walk in that freedom regardless of whether you are anointed and appointed or not—it comes with the package.

PRINCIPLE 2: THE ART OF PREPARATION

By its very nature, salvation is an ethereal concept. Often our experiences with God can be our greatest blessing or our greatest curse, pushing us up toward fresh revelation, or sinking us into maintaining a spiritual status quo. When we enter a new situation with a past revelation (of who God is and how He works), and the situation doesn't change the way we expect it to, then our situation can downgrade our revelation, and our experiences thereby affect our faith. We then tend to sink back to what our faith used to be, as opposed to allowing our revelation to hold the line and bolster our faith through hard times.

Let's say you're on a plane, and a snake gets loose in that plane. What do you do?

Let me tell you what you do—you take the plane up higher.

The reason eagles put their nests so high up in the mountains is that snakes can't survive in high altitudes. An eagle will swoop down and grab a snake, and take it up to an altitude where the snake cannot exist. It *literally* implodes because of the high air pressure.

Snakes operate in one plane, and eagles in another. The snake cannot function where the eagle nests. What you have to realize is that, like the eagle, you have to move the war to a different place. If you try to fight a snake on the ground, it has the ability to strike quickly. But once you take a snake high up into the sky, you have the advantage. The snake cannot exist in a place where you can exist. So you've got to move the battle to the place where you will win every time, because no snake can survive there. Your key to spiritual victory is to change the battlefield.

God does not function in the area of your sensory perceptions.

The Bible says no man has ever seen or touched God. I have never put my hands physically on God. You can't smell God. I don't know what kind of cologne He wears or what kind of soap He uses. No one knows these types of sensory things about God. If I live my life sensorially and sensually, then I will continually seek to validate what I believe about God through my life experiences. And if those don't line up, then I will struggle with trying to have a revelation of God that exceeds what my mind can conceive.

He does not work in a sensual world; He does not work according to my sensory data. His walk with me is not based on what I can see, because I walk by faith and not by sight. Therefore, I may not see anything God is doing. I may not be able to discern what He's doing, but if I have faith in the revelation of who God is, then my expectation is set at a good place.

My revelation cannot be deduced. It cannot be matriculated. It cannot be educated. It cannot be something I can fathom and process with my reason.

> **Ephesians 6:10-18**
> **Finally, my brethren, be strong in the Lord, and in the power of his might. Put on the whole armour of God, that ye may be able to stand against the wiles of the devil. For we wrestle not against flesh and blood, but against principalities, against powers, against the rulers of the darkness of this world, against spiritual wickedness IN HIGH PLACES. Wherefore take unto you the whole armour of God, that ye may be able to withstand in the evil day, and having done all, to stand. Stand therefore, having your loins girt about with truth, and having on the breastplate of righteousness; And your feet shod with the preparation of the gospel of peace; Above all, taking the shield of faith, wherewith ye shall be able to quench all the fiery darts of the wicked. And take the helmet of salvation, and the sword of the Spirit, which is the word of God: Praying always with all prayer and supplication in the Spirit, and watching thereunto with all perseverance and supplication for all saints.**

So Paul just shifted battlegrounds—that's right!

He just said, "You don't wrestle with flesh and blood, you wrestle with principalities and powers." If you fight the snake in the flesh, you'll lose! So I want you to shift your thinking. You cannot battle Satan in the natural. So don't live your life thinking he's not going to come. Put your nest high up in the mountains, so when you see him coming, you can grab him and take him into a place where the battleground shifts in your favor.

PRINCIPLE 2: THE ART OF PREPARATION

He can't fight you up there, because you wrestle not against flesh and blood, but against principalities and powers. Recognize who you are.

When I was a kid, we used to play a game called King of the Hill. One kid would run up to the top of the hill, and other kids would try to pull him off. The one who pulled him down would run up and become king of the hill.

Salvation means deliverance, healing, safety, protection, so you are not at the bottom of the hill, fighting to attack and get to the top. You are the one at the *top* of the hill. When God's Word tells you to stand, you stand against the wiles of the devil and his schemes and plans. You are literally pushing him down, saying, "You can't come up here! I'm holding the ground I was given. I'm not asking God to set me free—I am set free. I'm not asking Him to heal my body because I am healed. I don't ask Him to rescue me, because my loins are girded about with truth. I have the breastplate of righteousness. When you come against me, Satan, I'm not a defeated foe—I am already the king of the hill! I am standing against all your attacks."

Every weapon described here is defensive except for the sword of the spirit. Why?

Let's talk about the helmet of salvation. What does a helmet protect? Your head.

Everywhere you go, you go headfirst. When you were born, a few of y'all were stubborn and tried to come feet first, but you're *supposed* to come headfirst. From that point forward in your life, you've gone everywhere headfirst. So the helmet of salvation means what?

The faith that got you saved is the same faith that'll get you healed. It's the same faith that'll get you delivered. It's the same thing that'll set you up for success. It's the same faith. From the moment you got saved, when you first put on the helmet of salvation, when lying Satan said you're going to drown? You could say, "What are you talking about? I'm on top of the hill already! I'm the head and not the tail! I'm above and not beneath. Are you kidding me?"

The problem is, if you're not wearing your helmet of salvation, you'll begin to believe everything. Next thing you know, you'll be down there wondering why you're getting whooped.

God doesn't tell you to attack and take, yet he tells you to hold. Be like *antihistamine* and "stand against."

The battle is already won! The victory is already yours. Satan will try to twist you into believing you've got to fight to prosper, you've got to fight to get healed, you've got to fight to have salvation, you've got to fight to be rescued, you've got to fight to be delivered.

You will never experience victory until you stop focusing on your condition and begin realizing what your position is. Stop letting the snake pull you down. Remember you're an eagle and yank him up into your sky.

If I walk into a store and find somebody's got a problem with me—I've got plenty of money! I will spend it somewhere else. I can say, "You're not hurting my feelings; I ain't mad at you! You keep on with your demonic self."

PRINCIPLE 3

THE ART *of* FAITH

THY ENEMY'S WARFARE IS ALWAYS BASED ON DECEPTION.

Deception is your enemy's greatest weapon. When you understand and begin to recognize biblical truth, then you stack the odds against your enemy.

> **Ephesians 6:10-17**
> **Finally, my brethren, be strong in the Lord, and in the power of his might. Put on the whole armour of God, that ye may be able to stand against the wiles of the devil. For we wrestle not against flesh and blood, but against principalities, against powers, against the rulers of the darkness of this world, against spiritual wickedness in high places. Wherefore take unto you the whole armour of God, that ye may be able to withstand in the evil day, and having done all, to stand. Stand therefore, having your loins girt about with truth, and having on the breastplate of righteousness; And your feet shod with the preparation of the gospel of peace; Above all, taking the shield of faith, wherewith ye shall be able to quench all the fiery darts of the wicked. And take the helmet of salvation, and the sword of the Spirit, which is the word of God.**
>
> **Luke 22:31-32**
> **And the Lord said, Simon, Simon, behold, Satan hath desired to have you, that he may sift you as wheat: But I have prayed for thee, that thy faith fail not: and when thou art converted, strengthen thy brethren.**

These scriptures tell us that Satan is not after anything but your faith. He's not after your stuff—you are the only one who wants your stuff.

Because the Bible was written in ancient Hebrew and Greek, one of the challenges of proper biblical interpretation is discerning the meaning of certain words. For example, "love" is not always the same word in the Bible. You can love your dog, just don't *love* your dog. Even though the word "love" is used in our English Bibles, it doesn't have the same meaning in every place. In the Hebrew and Greek languages, different words for "love" have different connotations.

This is not a Bible college lesson. But have you ever heard a particular scripture or concept over and over, and then one day you went, "Aha, I got it"? All of a sudden something clicked, and it made sense. That's knowing something by discernment or by spiritual comprehension.

Sometimes you might deal with a person going through a type of problem you've experienced. You might say, "Look, I'm not telling you what I *heard*; I'm telling you what I *know*. I've been through that. Got the T-shirt and retired from it. I'm trying to help you, and I'm not speaking out of my comprehension—I speak from personal experience."

In the Sermon on the Mount, Jesus said that when He returns, He'll tell many people who claim to have done works in His name, "Depart from me, I never knew you" (Matthew 7:23). What He meant was "We haven't had any experience together. I know who you are, but you and I don't work together."

Right before the Last Supper, Peter and the other disciples were over there arguing about who was the greatest. And Jesus said, "Look, Peter, let me share something with you. Satan has asked for you, just put in a request for you by name. So what I'm going to tell you is, since I'm, you know, *God in the flesh* and I'm the creator of all things great and small, I'm the Alpha and the Omega, I'm just going to go ahead and rebuke that and shut it down."

OK, that's not what he said.

He gave Peter the typical church answer: "Oh, I'll pray for you, brother."

PRINCIPLE 3: THE ART OF FAITH

Jesus Himself.

I'd have been like, "Really? Jesus, you'll pray for me. Wow, I appreciate that. But, uh, since you beheld Satan fall from heaven like lightning, you were there when that happened...."

We Christians rally around salvation, getting saved, entering into the family of God—but very few people talk about the conversion process. When Jesus told Peter, "When thou art converted," He wasn't speaking about salvation. When Jesus asked, "Who do men say that I am," Peter was the one who stepped up and said, "Thou art the Christ, the son of the living God, God in the flesh."

Flesh and blood did not reveal that to Peter. So here we sit with a man who knows who Christ is. He is fully aware of his salvation that is vested in Christ. It is not now for him to determine what Christ is, because he already knows. It cannot be that this conversion process is about Peter getting saved or coming to the knowledge of Christ—he already came to that knowledge.

Jesus is like, "You guys are wondering who is the greatest, and all this other stuff, but Satan has asked for you. And since he's asked for you, I know he's coming for you. Since he's coming for you, I'm going to pray that your faith doesn't fail you, because when you're converted, I want you to turn around and strengthen your brother."

And Peter's first answer is "I will follow you into prison and to death" (Luke 22:33).

Yeah, whatever, Peter—them's lies!

I fully believe that at the time, Peter thought that was the truth. But we all know that's not what happened.

Jesus said, "Peter, the cock shall not crow this day before you have three times denied that you know me. You will deny that you even have a revelation of who I am. You will literally lose the revelation of who I am" (Luke 22:34).

Why does Satan want your faith? Theologian Paul Tillich said that the nature of faith transforms a finite being into an infinite reality. You need to understand that faith is the ultimate leveler. In this world, a particular talent may be distributed all around the globe, but an opportunity is not. You might have plenty of talented people in the hood, but because they don't have an opportunity, they can't capitalize on that talent.

I have known drug dealers who had greater leadership skills than some CEOs. But the socioeconomic conditions in which they were raised shifted their lives in a direction that denied them the opportunity to capitalize on those skills in a legitimate way.

Faith holds no gender. Faith holds no race. Faith is all about God, who is the ultimate leveler of the playing field, our opportunities—a finite reality. But when faith steps into the scene, it takes the finite and moves it into the world of infinite possibilities and dreams—the ultimate level.

> **Romans 12:3**
> **For I say, through the grace given unto me, to every man that is among you, not to think of himself more highly than he ought to think; but to think soberly, according as God hath dealt to every man the measure of faith.**

In other words, the more a person looks with the eyes of faith beyond what they can see in a natural sense, the more power becomes available to that person.

People ask, "Does faith conflict with natural law? Does faith conflict with my circumstance? Does faith conflict with reason? Aren't you in denial of reality when you make outlandish faith-based statements?"

None of this is the case, because faith is not in conflict with these things. Faith *transcends* these things. You and I can be in the same place at the same time and experience different things, because my faith is a place where I will not be handicapped by your limitations. I will not be shut down by *your* view of God; my revelation of God is individual to me. And if I believe that He's able, He can make it happen.

PRINCIPLE 3: THE ART OF FAITH

Why do so many people struggle with faith? If faith truly has the ability to do anything, then faith cannot be obtained by only certain individual parts of a person's body. It must be obtained by all your faculties.

You cannot have faith in your spirit and not have faith in your mind, your soul, and your body.

The nature of faith is not an intellectual discourse. It is based on probabilities; it's not gambling.

It's not looking at circumstances and saying, "Well, the odds are that I'm going to get through this. The odds are that this is not going to take me out. The odds are that nobody ever dies from a headache." Lots of people see faith that way.

The function or discourse or rule or law of nature is not faith, either.

For instance, you've probably gotten sick, and a doctor prescribed antibiotics. Now, if we beat the tree long enough, we can conclude that God gave man the knowledge to make antibiotics. We can, but quit saying that's God, because that's a rule or a function of nature.

If you were stuck in a two-story building, and you jumped out of it to deliver yourself from a fire and you maybe broke a leg, but you lived?

"Glory to God, I made it!!"

Look, I'm all about giving God the glory, but don't call that faith.

If you jumped out of *100 stories* and got up and walked away from it, *that* we can call faith, because that is not the natural course of the world.

Stop attributing things to God that are not altogether Him. That just limits your ability to delve into faith by depending on what you *see*. We don't walk by sight; we walk by faith in the Son of God who loved us.

The world can be a very different place for different people, based on the level of faith in which they are walking.

The first person to know the ending of any book is its author. As you read the book, its plot unfolds with many dips and turns. You are caught in a maze, on a trail predestinated by the author, and the only one who does not know where you're about to end up is you! So the writer is the author and finisher of that book, because he takes you to the finish line, to whatever end he has predetermined.

Spiritual victory is not a probability. It's not statistical. It's not based on something that is already happening or an assumption of the intellect. People who are ruled by their intellect have a problem with faith. Their intellectual capacity limits their outlook on life and directs what they're going to do in any given situation.

They say, "Well, I don't think I can afford to do that. I don't think that's gonna work for me. I'm not going to get that job because it's too far beyond my scope or my capabilities. I don't think I can do this. I'm not sure we can have that. I'm not sure God would bless this. I'm not sure He can heal this because nobody has gotten healed from this before today." (Interestingly, you could say the same about every athlete who has ever broken a record.)

The world of infinite possibilities has to be placed where it does not *conflict* with reason, but it just *transcends* reason. In other words, just because you *think* it's not possible that doesn't mean it is not possible.

A history teacher told the class to draw a picture of a historical event. As the teacher walks around, she looks at one little girl's picture and says, "What is that?"

The little girl says, "It's a whale."

The teacher asks, "What's this little person right here?"

"That's Jonah in the whale!"

The teacher says, "No, no sweetheart. I want you to draw a *historical, factual* event, something real that has happened."

The little girl says, "That did happen. The Bible says it happened."

The teacher says, "Oh no, sweetheart, it didn't happen."

PRINCIPLE 3: THE ART OF FAITH

The little girl says, "I'm telling you, it happened! When I get to heaven, I'm going to talk to him about it."

The teacher says, "What if he's not in heaven?"

The little girl says, "Then you ask him."

Faith and God are not confined by the parameters of your history and your science.

Think about it: Much of what you struggle with is not the absence of faith, but the presence of the wrong *type* of faith.

Faith is merely what you believe. As long as you hold on to your old, preconceived version of faith, new faith will never come along. The nature of your faith is vested in your ability to think, to process, to discern, and to know. And if what you know is based on your years of experience?

"You don't understand, Pastor, I've been dealing with sick folks all my life."

OK, let's take your little 40 or 50 years and compare that to the infinite position of God.

You think you know better than He does because, in some way, shape, or form, the narcissism in you has allowed you to think that you can even mentally process God in the first place.

Faith is the substance of things hoped for, the evidence of things not seen. It is proof of what I cannot see because it has not manifested yet in the realm of the natural, but I have it in the realm of the spirit. Everything in this world started with an idea. Whatever you're currently seated on started in somebody's head. It was conceived with something *not* seen in order to produce that which *is* seen.

People pray, "God, give me a car; give me a house; give me this …." God doesn't make cars or houses! He makes the metal that's in the ground. He makes the wood that's in the tree. And He expects you to come with a supply of faith to turn that resource into manifestation.

In a world of infinite possibilities, should I walk up to a tree and say, "No one's ever created a chair, so I guess the world will have to sit on the floor for the rest of eternity"?

Why do you deal with God that way?

What begins the realm of impossibility for you? It is not faith.

Everything functions by faith.

A recent article in a gossip publication describes disgraced comedian Bill Cosby trying to hide his money in Bitcoin because he believes his wife may leave him when he's incarcerated for his conviction as a sex offender.

According to an unnamed source, Cosby decided to try to invest his money in Bitcoin because then his US dollars disappear and only he can get access to his fortune.

Now the challenge with that is, number one: it's insane.

But number two: What do you think happens when he tries to do the impossible? He can't spend drachma. People want to be paid in US dollars!

The type of currency a buyer can use to purchase something is predicated upon what the seller will accept.

If you want to operate in the natural and deal with the natural, then live there. But if you want to transcend what is natural, what is expected or what is "normal" then you'd better understand that the currency of heaven is not in what God cannot do, but in what He *can* do. This might mess with you a little bit, because you spend all your life believing certain things.

When my daughter was learning how to dive into the pool (she already knew how to swim, how to float and stuff), she just jumped off the edge and into the water—no fear! One day, we were inside sitting on the couch, and she climbed up onto the ottoman and said, "Ready…Go!"

PRINCIPLE 3: THE ART OF FAITH

We were wondering what happened to "Set." If she had said "Set" after "Ready," we would have had enough time to catch her. But she skipped "Set" and went straight to "Go!"

Needless to say, she face-planted.

My point is that everything doesn't work everywhere.

She was only 20 months old. What's your excuse?

There are rules, and Satan wants your faith because your faith allows you access to transcend even him.

> **Luke 22:31-32**
> **And the Lord said, Simon, Simon, behold, Satan hath desired to have you, that he may sift you as wheat: But I have prayed for thee, that thy faith fail not: and when thou art converted, strengthen thy brethren.**

In our society, if you want flour, you just go down to Safeway and buy yourself a 5-pound or 10-pound bag. But back in ancient Israel, there was no Safeway.

In order to get grain, farmers had to beat wheat with a stick repeatedly to break off the kernels. They would winnow it on a windy day. The wind would blow away the unnecessary parts. Then they had to sort through it and pick out the dirt, bugs, and other impurities.

It's kinda like when you buy a bag of beans. (I hate beans, by the way.) If you're gonna cook some beans, you'd better sort through them, or you might not see a little pebble that *looked* like a bean, and ultimately end up at the dentist's office.

So they had to sort through and pick out the impurities. Then once they finished, the wheat had to be milled and ground. Finally, they'd have flour.

Beaten through the storm, all the impurities picked over, then ground up in order to be used. Yet all the stuff the wheat goes through isn't what transforms it into flour. What gets the wheat to the place it needs to be is its response to the attack it must endure in order to become what it needs to become.

You ought to rejoice that you have a reputation in hell.

You ought to rejoice that Satan is going, "Oh yeah, that one right there ... yeah, we're coming. We're coming for you."

You should be like, "What's up? Get at me, Bro!"

Why? Because the reality is that from the moment you are converted, "converted" no longer means "salvation." It means that when you get to the other side of the attack, you will be better equipped to handle the responsibility God places on your life. People tend to complain about it! Complaining is not faith.

God is waiting for you to get to the place where you understand that He is able to bring you through the attack. That's why the Bible says that faith is able to quench the fiery darts of the enemy.

Do you know what a fiery dart is? It's an arrow that has been specially dressed on the end so it can be lighted on fire. What's the point?

When it lands, it sparks a blaze. The shield of faith can stop those darts. And you need it because the enemy is always throwing something.

Let's say you know you messed up. If you let that mess-up hit you, it'll spark a blaze inside you. All of a sudden you'll be thinking more about what you did wrong than what you have done right. You will begin to forget what God is trying to do because you have dropped your shield of faith and allowed yourself to be exposed to the fiery darts of the enemy.

The enemy is constantly wailing those fiery darts at you to see if you're willing to give up your shield of faith.

Jesus said, "I pray for you that your faith fails not, and when you are converted, strengthen your brother."

The first thing Peter said was, "Lord, I'm ready to go with you to prison."

PRINCIPLE 3: THE ART OF FAITH

Let me explain something to you. Usually, the person who jumps up and says what they're gonna do is the person that ain't going to do it!

I've been in ministry for almost 15 years, and it's amazing to me how new people come to church and they have to meet with the pastor. They've got to come talk to me and tell me how great the message was. Those are the ones I know we probably won't see again.

Here Jesus was already tapping into some problems with Peter. Peter's immediate response was very prideful, but Jesus knew that was not going to happen.

What do you do when you've got someone flawed like Peter?

He's the one with a revelation that Jesus is, in fact, the Son of the living God.

What do you do with someone like Peter, who is constantly opening his mouth and inserting his foot?

What do you do with a person like Peter who, if you push him too far, will cut you?

You may not be able to relate to Peter, but I can relate to this man. This man is helping me to understand that I might not be perfect. I might not have it all together, but my God can use me to do great things even though I might not be what you would call refined.

Peter did cut somebody—cut him deep.

It takes a God who is rich in mercy to look at a man like Peter and be like, "I know what you're gonna do." Do you think Jesus was surprised? He wasn't. He said, "You'll deny me three times"—yet He still loved him.

In the same situation, Satan entered Judas's heart to betray Jesus. Both men were picked by Jesus. Both were sitting at the same table. The difference between the two was in how they responded to the attack.

Jesus looked at Judas and said, "That thing you're about to do? Hurry up."

He looked at Peter and said, "Satan is after you, but I'll pray that your faith doesn't fail now. This joker, Judas, his faith already failed him, so he's already off and running—he's about to do what I need him to do."

Can you imagine being regulated like Peter was and still acting like an idiot?

Do you know what that tells me? There's room for me, that's what it tells me.

It tells me that no matter what, when Satan comes and starts telling me about my past, I've got to remind him of his future. I don't have to be afraid. I don't have to be scared. I don't have to run from the attack.

The moment you get through it, the moment you get to the other side, your job is to turn around and strengthen your brethren. Your job is to help somebody else, because now you're prepared. You are equipped. You know what to do and how to do it. Now you're ready.

You are not ready because you confessed: "I love God." You are not ready because you have just come into the household of God. You are ready when you have taken some hits, had some punches and some kicks, when you've been through some stuff.

There are people in your life you're going to have to let go of, because they're deceived. Satan wages his battle through deceptions that constantly come at you, and these people are the wielders of fiery darts. I'm challenging you to understand how war is waged. I want you to question Satan more than you question God.

What's the point of what you can do if you never will do it?

PRINCIPLE 4: THE ART OF AUTHORITY

How do you bind a demon that a person wants to keep around? You don't have authority in other people's lives; you have authority in yours. I cannot tell you that Satan is not allowed to come and mess with you and your mind and everything concerning you—but I can tell you he can't come to my house!

Some people flirt with and play with the very thing they don't want, then complain when they get it. Strange, isn't it?

> **Luke 10:19**
> **Behold, I give unto you power to tread on serpents and scorpions, and over all the power of the enemy: and nothing shall by any means hurt you.**

When you see "serpent" and "scorpion" in scripture, you should read "devils" and "demons." Serpents and scorpions are scriptural codewords referring to demons and devils.

People mistakenly believe every satanic attack is overt. They are not overt. Satan uses strategies and plans. If he can't get to you, he will tag those closest to you.

You must be extremely careful with people who only want to be next to you—not because they want to bring a supply to you, but because they want something from you. They're out to take, not to give. You have to be careful with certain types of people and their ways of thinking and functioning. Even if they say they are a Christian, that does not mean they are not operating under evil influences.

Jesus said, "Behold, I give you authority (or power or mastery) to tread on serpents and scorpions and over all the ability of the enemy." So why would Paul need to say in Ephesians that we wrestle not against flesh and blood, but against principalities and powers? Why should we have to wrestle with that over which we already have power and authority?

Just because you have a legal right to authority doesn't mean you exercise it.

Mark Twain is attributed with saying that a man who doesn't read has no significant advantage over a man who *can't* read.

So quit thinking that just because you know you *have* authority, you actually *operate* in it. A person who has authority and doesn't operate in it is no better than a person who doesn't have it. Such a person does not battle in the divine providence of God.

When I was in high school, before Christ was in my life, my friends had some kind of beat-up car—something kind of small—and eight or nine of us would get together and move the car. We would literally pick that puppy up! We'd shimmy it this way and that way, we'd put it sideways and all kinds of stuff. Now, listen, no way could I do that by myself. But if I garner enough people with the ability, I can do anything.

When it comes to moving something, that's called leverage. I can try to move a big boulder by pushing it, and not get it to budge. But I can jam a hard piece of wood under it and use my full body weight as leverage and make it move.

Currently, we can put my youngest child into a playpen and she cannot get out. Even if she had an elephant in the playpen with her, she could not escape that thing. She'd have power, but her knowledge is limited.

A moment will come when she figures out leverage. Then she'll see she has an advantage! It will help her do what she cannot do in her limited strength.

If I'm wrestling, then I am engaged by things that are trying to hurt me. I can also be engaged by people who want to hurt me and by things that are trying to steal my faith.

God has not taken out of the world every single thing that will come against your life. But He wants you to know that whatever the ability of the enemy is, whatever his strategy, whatever his scheme, you have the victory over it. God has given you authority or mastery over the enemy's ability.

PRINCIPLE 4: THE ART OF AUTHORITY

If you have mastery over Satan's ability, then your authority must be rooted in the One who gave it to you.

As you deal with Satan, who is talking—you or God? Because if it's *you* talking, then Satan has no desire or responsibility to deal with what you said.

And then people wonder why they're being ignored, right?

See, the value of the authority is based on the one who gives it. Jesus lets you know that if you function in the power of His might, that power doesn't originate from you. It comes from Him.

Even if you don't think you have authority, you still have it. Whether or not you *believe* God has given you authority does not change the fact you have it. Your belief affects whether or not you *function* in it, and how much mastery you exercise over the ability.

So then can the enemy hurt you? Yes. Yes, he can.

Can he trip you up? Yes, he can.

Your ability does not come from knowing what authority is. It's in your revelation of having that authority.

> **Ephesians 1:1-6**
> **Paul, an apostle of Jesus Christ by the will of God, to the saints which are at Ephesus, and to the faithful in Christ Jesus: Grace be to you, and peace, from God our Father, and from the Lord Jesus Christ. Blessed be the God and Father of our Lord Jesus Christ, who hath blessed us with all spiritual blessings in heavenly places in Christ: According as he hath chosen us in him before the foundation of the world, that we should be holy and without blame before him in love: Having predestinated us unto the adoption of children by Jesus Christ to himself, according to the good pleasure of his will, To the praise of the glory of his grace, wherein he hath made us accepted in the beloved.**

Let's be very, very clear about who Paul is writing to here: he's writing to the church, to the saints, to the believers at Ephesus, and to whomever else believes. That makes this letter not only to the Church of Ephesus, but also to the church *here*—it's still important!

It doesn't say that He *will* bless us; it says He *hath*.

So when did He do it? It's already done!

You have been predestinated.

Some people are confused about destiny. They think destiny means that God has a detailed plan for their life and they are just drones rolling in a world over which they have no control. That's not it. "Predestinated" means that God has a plan for your life that is very specific to *God*, but seems nebulous or ethereal to *you*—like a vapor or smoke. You have to work to achieve or understand what that will is concerning your life.

If God says He has already given you (or blessed you) with all spiritual blessings, he is not praying you would get blessed. Too many believers talk like that: "I'm praying that you get blessed. Lord, bless them!"

Bless them with what? If He has given us all spiritual blessing, what in the world are you talking about?

We already have all spiritual blessing, so the primary focus is to get hot after God, to chase after Him. As you increase in your revelation, you will increase in your role according to what He gave you.

Just because you're in church does not mean you are a Christian. There are many people in the church who aren't! Do they even believe the revelation?
Sometimes you'll deal with people and they'll be like, "I'm believing for my healing. I'm just waiting on my healing!"

I'm like, what are you waiting on? You are preaching a different doctrine. We're waiting on *you* to come into the fullness of the revelation in the knowledge of Him.

Interestingly, Paul said, "I'm praying for you. I'm praying that you have every blessing and that you come to the fullness of the revelation of who

PRINCIPLE 4: THE ART OF AUTHORITY

God is so that as you come to the revelation and the knowledge of Him, the eyes of your understanding may become enlightened."

It is not about whether you have it or don't have it; it's about *knowing* you have it. This is why you are either going to walk in it or you aren't, which comes down to the very rudimentary aspect of faith.

Faith in itself means to have what you do not see. It's believing in what you cannot tangibly put your hands on, but you believe it anyway.

> **1 John 4:4**
> **Ye are of God, little children, and have overcome them: because greater is he that is in you, than he that is in the world.**

So as you're faced with something, you'll say, "Greater is He that is in me than he that is in the world, and I can overcome that! I'm greater than that. I can get this thing, I can buy that house, get that new car, I can do this thing, I can get that new job."

Here's the problem: That's not what Paul is talking about.

This is one of those places where Christians like to grab on the soundbites; they pick out little pieces because they sound good.

> **1 John 4:1**
> **Beloved, believe not every spirit, but try the spirits whether they are of God: because many false prophets are gone out into the world.**

What is the subject matter here?

Spirits that are not of God: demons, scorpions, serpents.

Stop talking like this verse is empowerment for you to go get a new job, because that's not what it means (although it might!) That's good, but the greater issue is that I have overcome the spirits in the world, because greater is the One who gave me authority!

> **1 Samuel 17:2-9**
> And Saul and the men of Israel were gathered together, and pitched by the valley of Elah, and set the battle in array against the Philistines. And the Philistines stood on a mountain on the one side, and Israel stood on a mountain on the other side: and there was a valley between them. And there went out a champion out of the camp of the Philistines, named Goliath, of Gath, whose height was six cubits and a span. And he had an helmet of brass upon his head, and he was armed with a coat of mail; and the weight of the coat was five thousand shekels of brass. And he had greaves of brass upon his legs, and a target of brass between his shoulders. And the staff of his spear was like a weaver's beam; and his spear's head weighed six hundred shekels of iron: and one bearing a shield went before him. And he stood and cried unto the armies of Israel, and said unto them, Why are ye come out to set your battle in array? am not I a Philistine, and ye servants to Saul? choose you a man for you, and let him come down to me. If he be able to fight with me, and to kill me, then will we be your servants: but if I prevail against him, and kill him, then shall ye be our servants, and serve us.

Goliath was almost 10 feet tall. He wore a brass helmet and was armored with a coat of mail that weighed 5,000 shekels of brass, which means it was between *150 to 200 pounds*. That was about how much David weighed *in* the armor he wore!

> **1 Samuel 17:10-20**
> And the Philistine said, I defy the armies of Israel this day; give me a man, that we may fight together. When Saul and all Israel heard those words of the Philistine, they were dismayed, and greatly afraid. Now David was the son of that Ephrathite of Bethlehemjudah, whose name was Jesse; and he had eight sons: and the man went among men for an old man in the days of Saul. And the three eldest sons of Jesse went and followed Saul to the battle: and the names of his three sons that went to the battle were Eliab the firstborn, and next unto him Abinadab, and the third Shammah. And David was the youngest: and the three eldest followed Saul. But David went and returned from Saul to feed his father's sheep at Bethlehem. And the Philistine drew near morning and evening, and presented himself forty days. And Jesse

PRINCIPLE 4: THE ART OF AUTHORITY

> said unto David his son, Take now for thy brethren an ephah of this parched corn, and these ten loaves, and run to the camp of thy brethren; And carry these ten cheeses unto the captain of their thousand, and look how thy brethren fare, and take their pledge. Now Saul, and they, and all the men of Israel, were in the valley of Elah, fighting with the Philistines. And David rose up early in the morning, and left the sheep with a keeper, and took, and went, as Jesse had commanded him; and he came to the trench, as the host was going forth to the fight, and shouted for the battle.

Jesse told David, "Take some food out to your brothers on the battlefield."

David rose up early in the morning, leaving the sheep with a keeper, and he did as Jesse had commanded him. He came to a trench where the Philistines had put the battle in array, army against army. David left his carriage, ran to the army, and found his brother. While they were talking, here came the Philistine champion, Goliath of Gath, marching out of the army of the Philistines. David watched the Israelite soldiers flee from this man when they saw him.

The men of Israel were so afraid, they said, "Have you seen this man that comes out with such confidence to defy Israel? The king will give great riches to the man who kills him, including his daughter, and will make all his family members free in Israel!"

David spoke up and said, "Whoa, whoa, whoa, wait, wait, wait, hold on! *What* would be done to the dude who kills this guy?"

The army of Israel was being threatened, and they were all afraid. Goliath was screaming, "I came to kill the army of Israel!"

David called him an uncircumcised Philistine.

In today's modern world, we think of circumcision as a certain procedure involving the member of a male's body, right? But in Old Testament times, to call somebody "uncircumcised" meant they were outside God's *covenant* with Israel. Circumcision was the sign of the covenant God made with Abraham.

So when David called Goliath an "uncircumcised Philistine," he was really saying "How dare this non-covenant person come against God's covenant!"

> **1 Samuel 17:28-30**
> **And Eliab his eldest brother heard when he spake unto the men; and Eliab's anger was kindled against David, and he said, Why camest thou down hither? and with whom hast thou left those few sheep in the wilderness? I know thy pride, and the naughtiness of thine heart; for thou art come down that thou mightest see the battle. And David said, What have I now done? Is there not a cause? And he turned from him toward another, and spake after the same manner: and the people answered him again after the former manner.**

The Bible says David left his sheep with the keeper, so he didn't abandon them in the wilderness. But his older brother is calling David's character into question.

He says, "The only reason you're here is you want to see what's going on!"

David responds, "What have I done now? What do you have a problem with? I'm here bringing you all food. Dad sent me. You're over here running from this uncircumcised Philistine, and you've got the nerve to accuse me of naughtiness in my heart!" Typical little brother. I was the youngest in my family, I can relate!

> **1 Samuel 17:31-32**
> **And when the words were heard which David spake, they rehearsed them before Saul: and he sent for him. And David said to Saul, Let no man's heart fail because of him; thy servant will go and fight with this Philistine.**

David said, "The Lord delivered me out of the hands of the bear and out of the paw of the lion. The Lord is the one who fought that battle, and He will do the same thing with this Philistine right here, so don't be afraid! I'm going to go out there and handle this thing, since y'all said I'm going to be rich! I get your daughter and my whole family gets set free? Dude, you have *no idea* what we're fitting to do."

PRINCIPLE 4: THE ART OF AUTHORITY

Goliath said, "You sent this little boy with a stick to come and mess with me? Are y'all crazy?"

> **1 Samuel 17:47**
> **And all this assembly shall know that the Lord saveth not with sword and spear: for the battle is the Lord's, and he will give you into our hands."**

God has uniquely made you with innate skills that you have tested and proved. God has developed you over time to be able to stand before *any giants*.

Start telling the giant how big your God is!

When God is in your life, he has already given you the authority and the ability to deal with a giant. Quit trying to pick up somebody else's armor. Quit looking at somebody else and trying to be like them. Quit trying to be something that you are not. You have a uniqueness in you, and God will use what is already in you. David didn't need a sword and he didn't notice the weapon that was forged against him. *David won before he got on the battlefield.*

Many people are afraid before the battle even starts. They pray out of fear, not out of faith. But if you pray out of *faith*, then you'll start commanding things to happen! Your revelation has got to come to the point where you have the victory before you even step out to fight.

Winning is not done on the battlefield; Winning was done before I even got there.

THE ART OF WAR

Principle 5

THE ART *of* COURAGE

IF THY WILL FACE THY FEAR, EVEN UNTO DEATH, THERE IS NOTHING THOU WILL NOT ACHIEVE.

Mark 8:27-38
And Jesus went out, and his disciples, into the towns of Caesarea Philippi: and by the way he asked his disciples, saying unto them, Whom do men say that I am? And they answered, John the Baptist; but some say, Elias; and others, One of the prophets. And he saith unto them, But whom say ye that I am? And Peter answereth and saith unto him, Thou art the Christ. And he charged them that they should tell no man of him. And he began to teach them, that the Son of man must suffer many things, and be rejected of the elders, and of the chief priests, and scribes, and be killed, and after three days rise again. And he spake that saying openly. And Peter took him, and began to rebuke him. But when he had turned about and looked on his disciples, he rebuked Peter, saying, Get thee behind me, Satan: for thou savourest not the things that be of God, but the things that be of men. And when he had called the people unto him with his disciples also, he said unto them, Whosoever will come after me, let him deny himself, and take up his cross, and follow me. For whosoever will save his life shall lose it; but whosoever shall lose his life for my sake and the gospel's, the same shall save it. For what shall it profit a man, if he shall gain the whole world, and lose his own soul? Or what shall a man give in exchange for his soul? Whosoever therefore shall be ashamed of me and of my words in this adulterous and sinful generation; of him also shall the Son of man be ashamed, when he cometh in the glory of his Father with the holy angels.

Jesus is asking a question, and the question almost has to be rhetorical.

He says, "What is the profit for a man if he loses his soul while gaining the world?"

Can you lose your soul when you gain the world, or if you gain the world, do you *automatically* lose your soul? And at what point, while you are in the world, is your soul in jeopardy?

Do you just have to be aware and alert as to how to manage it all, to keep it balanced so that you can actually have the world and still save your soul? Or is he telling you that it is absolutely 100 percent just not possible?

Axioms are things that are stated that are not subject to debate.

The words Jesus spoke are not subject to debate, and so they are the truth that literally has to be perpetual for all eternity. An axiom cannot be refuted or denied, no matter how much eternity you put behind it; it's an absolute fact.

Eschatology is the study of the end times. I have often seen it related to the nature of what is called the "white throne judgement" versus the judgment seat of Christ. Briefly, there are two judgments that every single person on this planet will face. You either face the "white throne judgment," which is the judgment for those who don't believe in Christ, or you will face the judgment seat of Christ, at which you will be evaluated based on what you have done with the life God has given you as a believer.

In this context, we can see some things that help us to get more clarity regarding what Jesus means by what He says here.

If the wealth of the wicked is laid up for the just, then that would contradict the idea that we are not allowed to gain the wealth of the world? How are we going to fund the things that God wants to do if we are unable to gain the possessions of the world? If Jesus is saying that you cannot gain worldly possessions or wealth without losing your soul, that doesn't fit the context in which He was speaking.

Some Christians don't know what they believe anymore.

PRINCIPLE 5: THE ART OF COURAGE

Some Christians knew Jesus is the only way to heaven, and now they're unsure.

When faced with varying viewpoints of what God has or has not said, their reprobate mind begins purporting a gospel that is not, in fact, the *real gospel*.

The question then becomes whether or not gaining the world is based on winning the world. If you look up the word *gaining* here, it means "to win."

In other words, Jesus is saying, "If you win in the world's way, then you're going to have to lose your soul to do it."

It's a zero-sum game when it comes to dealing with the world. You either do it the world's way and win in a worldly way, or you do it God's way—and, in the mind of the world, you lose. Living God's way implies that you are a cult member. There's something wrong with you. You are unintelligent. How can an intelligent human being believe that some higher power created all this stuff? Intelligent people believe in science. And scientific facts show that the earth is x-number of years old, and prehistoric animals were x-number of years old based on carbon dating, which was devised by people to assess what they don't know. And somehow, we're supposed to rely on science over Christ, over what the Word tells us.

We are all born into the world having no notable distinction, no real identity. So it's possible for us to lose our identity in the world. We can be shaped by our environment and the influence of secular people around us.

In today's society, our children are taught that they can't be different—this is a problem. Our kids have to blend in; they have to fit. Having an idiosyncratic identity is frowned upon, and many seek to conform to this world. The best way to avoid being picked on or talked about is to succumb to peer pressure and make compromises. My child will have to learn that we live by a certain standard. We don't function this way just because you're a pastor's kid! We live unto God because we are Christians first. I know pastors who tell their children to act a certain way because they are in the ministry. This emphasis breeds contempt for the ministry. It promotes the idea that Christians can have loose morals as long as they are not in ministry. But the very core of who we all are as believers sets us at odds with the ways of the world.

Too many parents have sat by and allowed the world to dictate societal trends. Christians get too busy worrying about stupid stuff and not thinking about society's impact on their kids.

Our world needs Christian politicians! We need Christian business owners. We need some Christian billionaires writing checks to make some things change!

But instead of getting involved, we complain about the way the world is, and how bad it is.

Believers no longer have distinguishing characteristics. You can put a whole group of people in a room, or in a job, and you won't know which ones are Christians and which ones aren't.

They're all cussing together. They're all talking smack about their bosses together. When 5 p.m. comes around, they're all out the door. It takes at least five minutes to get your stuff together, which means you started out the door at 4:56!

So what makes you stand out in a crowd?

What makes you different when you don't function from a different set of beliefs?

If you have no identity or distinction from the world, then you have lost your identity in the world. Having lost your identity in the world, you take on what the world cares about. If you're not careful, you'll allow your experiences in the world to modify your expectation of God.

It's easy to lose your distinctive Christian identity in the world because of the tension, the constant pull toward a solidarity that comes with wanting to be in the world.

PRINCIPLE 5: THE ART OF COURAGE

A movie can tell a story in such a way that you're rooting for the bad guy. The guy might be a murderer. He's low-down dirty, but you want him to live. You want him to win at the end. You want him to get away with whatever he's doing.

That goes to show you that your basis of morality can be swayed by being entertained.

> **Mark 8:33-34**
> **But when he had turned about and looked on his disciples, he rebuked Peter, saying, Get thee behind me, Satan: for thou savourest not the things that be of God, but the things that be of men. And when he had called the people unto him with his disciples also, he said unto them, Whosoever will come after me, let him deny himself, and take up his cross, and follow me.**

Jesus had just finished explaining to them what was going to happen to Him and why His death was necessary to redeem mankind.

What's the subject matter? It's not death; it's following after Him!

Jesus is not talking about death, judgment and the final destiny of the soul and humankind here; He's talking about picking up your cross and following. It is disingenuous and fraudulent for you to be in the world and not rep who you really are!

People think that courage is the absence of fear, but the precursor to courage must *be* fear. You cannot have courage where there is no fear. Courage is not required to do the things you normally do. Being in the world and satiated with the things of the world takes no courage. Your Christianity doesn't make a difference in the world until you become different. Yet we've allowed our children to think it's not OK to be different, that they need to conform. Peer pressure says they need to conform!

The truth of the matter is you will not live until you become different.

Conformity and compromise lead to obscurity and obsolescence.

Stress and depression are rooted in one word: Agency. *Agency* simply means you have the ability to direct your life.

Hopelessness enters into people when they've lost a perception of agency. The only way you can be hopeless is if you feel that your life is no longer in control. And you can be depressed if you feel like you are not in control of whatever you are experiencing.

The relationship between agency and anxiety is very close. The less agency you have, the more anxiety you feel. Anxiety and depression are diametrically opposed to your agency.

> **Revelation 12:11**
> **And they overcame him by the blood of the Lamb, and by the word of their testimony; and they loved not their lives unto the death.**

The greatest weapon Satan can use in your life is the love of your life.

The blood of the lamb is the means by which we fight. The word of their testimony was their weapon, and they did not love their lives until death became the driving force.

How did we overcome by the blood of the lamb? What lamb? Jesus, what's our weapon?

The word of our testimony.

What comes out of your mouth? What is your driving force so that you love not your life?

Jesus said, "What point is it to be in the world, to mind the things of the world, when I brought you to be in the world to *affect* the world?"

The ultimate level of courage is to bring distinction to you regarding how you influence the world, having the courage to stand up for what is right in the midst of a culture that says anything goes.

PRINCIPLE 5: THE ART OF COURAGE

Satan was OK with you until you decided you were going to serve. Then Satan said, "Oh no you don't! Are you crazy? You're not going to serve in a house of God."

You were all right by Satan when you were just saved, hiding in the pew and doing absolutely nothing. But the moment you decided you're going to serve?

Satan said, "Oh no, we're not having that. Demons, attack them with something."

You are in the midst of such an attack because you decided to be different and have the courage to step up, to be counted, not to give in, to give up the world's way of doing things.

Peter thought he was doing the right thing. "Jesus, we won't let that happen to you!"

Jesus was like, "Dude, you savor the things of the world. You value life so much that you value life over redemption! I didn't come here to keep My life. I literally came here for the purpose of laying it down. I came here for the purpose of *dying* for this thing. If you're going to follow Me, you're going to have to pick up your cross. You're going to have to give up some stuff. You're going to have to make some commitments. If you're going to follow Me, you've got to get out of your own head; you've got to give up your plan. You might have to let go of some people. You're going to have to be alienated. If you're going to follow me, you're going to have to let go, to pick up your cross, and carry it all the way to the finish line. Pick up your cross and follow after Me."

Many historians believe that the cross Jesus carried weighed almost 150 pounds—that's the weight of a person! Jesus said to pick up the ultimate courage. Just overcome fear.

The Bible says we are salt and light. Did you notice that the salt was more important than the gold in that sentence? Salt was worth more than gold back then!

Why? Because they might have killed the cow on Tuesday, but they could not put that cow in the refrigerator! They didn't have one! So they ate until they got tired, and then they got their wives and kids, and everybody ate until they were tired. Then they had to figure out what to do with everything that was left—making jerky using salt as a preservative, because salt kills bacteria.

You weren't called to just fall into the background and be like everybody else. You were called to be salt!

What does that mean? It means that when you rub up against somebody evil, they start shriveling.

You're not called just to sit back and let the world do whatever it wants to do. You are salt! You are light! You're not supposed to become satiated with the rhythms of the world, the music of the world, because you are what you consume.

We're all flawed. I want you to understand that we're all flawed. But the reality is that when He said, "What is it for man to gain the world and to lose his soul," He was talking about how you live.

He's talking about whether or not you'll pick up your cross.

How do you live your life? What are you waiting for the courage to do?

I've been self-employed most of my professional career. I've had many different companies. I've sold some of them. Some are still in business today, and some didn't make it while I was at their helm.

If you're an entrepreneur, you're going to fail, and you're going to succeed. The goal is to succeed more than you fail.

My God is well in control. My God has all the answers. My God knows exactly what's happening right now. I trust in Him and know He's got me come what may. The powers that be can walk in here today and say, "Everybody's fired!" So what? You won't hold me hostage!

Some of you are ready to courage up and come out of your fears. Take a step into a place where we are salt and light. We are the people with the

PRINCIPLE 5: THE ART OF COURAGE

victory. We are the chosen generation. We are royal priests. We have a job, to function as a light; darkness cannot exist when we step on the scene! *Salt and light.*

Why do you allow your fears to let you ponder at the pool of popularity?

Every parent says at some point, "If your friends jumped off a bridge, would you do it, too?"

I don't know, will you?

It's not that you won't experience moments of fear; of course, there will be moments. But you can still move and be encouraged, even while you're afraid.

What are you doing with the life you've been given?

THE ART OF WAR

Principle 6

THE ART of COUNTERBALANCE STRATEGY

YOUR ENEMY'S GREATEST ATTACKS COME IN THE SEASONS THAT ARE MOST ADVANTAGEOUS TO HIM.

Luke 4:1-13
And Jesus being full of the Holy Ghost returned from Jordan, and was led by the Spirit into the wilderness, Being forty days tempted of the devil. And in those days he did eat nothing: and when they were ended, he afterward hungered. And the devil said unto him, If thou be the Son of God, command this stone that it be made bread. And Jesus answered him, saying, It is written, That man shall not live by bread alone, but by every word of God. And the devil, taking him up into an high mountain, shewed unto him all the kingdoms of the world in a moment of time. And the devil said unto him, All this power will I give thee, and the glory of them: for that is delivered unto me; and to whomsoever I will I give it. If thou therefore wilt worship me, all shall be thine. And Jesus answered and said unto him, Get thee behind me, Satan: for it is written, Thou shalt worship the Lord thy God, and him only shalt thou serve. And he brought him to Jerusalem, and set him on a pinnacle of the temple, and said unto him, If thou be the Son of God, cast thyself down from hence: For it is written, He shall give his angels charge over thee, to keep thee: And in their hands they shall bear thee up, lest at any time thou dash thy foot against a stone. And Jesus answering said unto him, It is said, Thou shalt not tempt the Lord thy God. And when the devil had ended all the temptation, he departed from him for a season.

Note that this passage says the devil departed from him for a season.

You need to understand that God operates in seasons. The Word refers to seasons in a variety of ways. It says that as long as the earth shall remain, there shall be seedtime and harvest—those are seasons. He likens them to day and night, winter, spring, fall, and summer. They always come with amazing regularity ... unless you live in Arizona, in which you have two seasons—hot and hotter!

Satan was there for a season, and then he departed from Jesus for another season. Jesus was going through the process. He had just been baptized in the preceding chapter, and now he was finding Himself under scrutiny in the wilderness. And as He went through those seasons or changes within His life, God brought revelation and affirmation to His followers regarding who Jesus really is. Until then, he was a carpenter. He was Mary's boy.

Now it was starting to become clear through revelation who Jesus really is. You have to understand that when revelation comes, Satan tries to move with it in order to bring an attack.

> **Matthew 4:11**
> **Then the devil leaveth him, and, behold, angels came and ministered unto him.**

In times of testing and attack, many people think it's natural forces at work because they see natural things, right? But no, we wrestle not against flesh and blood, but against principalities and powers. Wrestling against flesh and blood is simpler, because you either win because you're the strongest or you lose because you're the weakest. You can easily articulate whether or not you win based on parameters of which you're fully aware. But the moment you move beyond flesh and blood, you enter the realm of what you do not know. Who wins and who loses has nothing to do with your ability. The fight becomes transcendent, beyond abilities.

You can punch flesh and blood in the nose, but how do you give Satan a black eye?

Seasons only function in a natural state of time. When it comes to faith and to God and to His promises, most people have a problem: They struggle with time.

PRINCIPLE 6: THE ART OF COUNTERBALANCE STRATEGY

Time wasn't instituted until Adam sinned. Time is a measure that allows an expanse of space and duration to bring man back into reconciliation with God. Otherwise, Adam would have lived eternally in a fallen state, and so would all of mankind. Before Adam fell, time as we know it simply did not exist.

God lives in eternity. He does not have the same problems and challenges we have because we live in time. Living in time means we are ruled by a watch, clocks, and calendars. Therefore, faith becomes stretched in the presence of time. Time necessitates our waiting to believe on the eternal, which is how we know that the world was framed by things we're not seeing.

If you are waiting for something to happen, then you are not operating in faith; you are operating from a natural place. There's a season and a time to every purpose under heaven—a time to be born, a time to die, a time to plant, a time to pluck up that which is planted, a time to kill, a time to heal, a time to break down, a time to build up, a time to laugh, a time to mourn, a time to dance, a time to cast away stones, a time to gather stones together, a time to embrace, a time to refrain from embracing, a time to get, a time to lose, the time to keep, a time to cast away, and so on and so forth.

The Bible tells us the time for everything and refers to it as a season.

There are expanses of time when the Bible says "in due season, you shall reap" (Galatians 6:9). In other words, when you're trying to reach a goal and it's not happening as you envision it, you are trying to mix up God's seasons.

> **1 Chronicles 12:32**
> **And of the children of Issachar, which were men that had understanding of the times, to know what Israel ought to do; the heads of them were two hundred; and all their brethren were at their commandment.**

You've got to have a revelation of what and who God is. There's a shift that happens when revelation shows up. There's a moment where you've been coming to church and the pastor has been preaching about your prosperity, about your healing, about what belongs to you in Christ—then all of a sudden there comes a moment where it hits your ears a certain way and it leaves a residue on your psyche that changes your mind about what you believe.

> **1 Corinthians 16:9**
> **For a great door and effectual is opened unto me, and there are many adversaries.**

Many people try to let open doors be their leading.

In other words, just because so-and-so called and said that they're offering you a job, you'll go and say, "God opened the door!" The offering of the job was not God opening a door. If you follow the pattern biblically, you will see.

> **Revelation 3:8**
> **I know thy works: behold, I have set before thee an open door, and no man can shut it: for thou hast a little strength, and hast kept my word, and hast not denied my name.**

He's watching your behavior. He's watching your works. The thing that He sent before cannot be to *lead* you, it's got to be to *reward* you. He rewards you by promoting you to the next level. When you're about to shift, Satan steps in and puts adversaries at the door.

> **Mark 1:12-13**
> **And immediately the spirit driveth him into the wilderness. And he was there in the wilderness forty days, tempted of Satan; and was with the wild beasts; and the angels ministered unto him.**

Jesus was in the wilderness. I think people are not aware of what "wilderness" was and have become desensitized to the meaning of the word "wilderness." You might say "I'm kind of stuck in the wilderness right now. I'm trying to figure myself out." Jesus was in the middle of a place where wild beasts were trying to kill him. He was laying his head

PRINCIPLE 6: THE ART OF COUNTERBALANCE STRATEGY

down in a place where he could be bitten by snakes. You've probably seen lions and tigers and bears, but you have seen them in their captive state where they're getting fed a balanced diet, and they have a place to sleep!

Here, Jesus is surviving in the wilderness, and along comes Satan.

First, he attacks Jesus' appetite: "Since you're so hungry, if you're really the Son of God, just command some bread into existence!"

Next, he attacks His ambition: "If you'll worship me, I can give you all the power in the world and then some!" And with that, he attacks Jesus' ability to obtain what He already knew He was going to get.

Which leads us to the third temptation: avoidance, the avoidance of work, the avoidance of effort. "I'll give you this power so you don't have to work hard. I'll help you avoid three years of ministry. I'll help you so that you can have what your ambition wants you to have."

Whatever you lack, Satan will use to bait you. Whatever you desire and want *so badly*, Satan will use to mess with you.

Jesus went through a process of being baptized and scrutinized then galvanized. *Galvanized* means "to shock into action." He was born; He was baptized in the Holy Ghost, confirmed, and scrutinized. He had to be evaluated because if He is, in fact, who He says He is, then He ought to be able to stand any test Satan could throw His way. Once He proved His authority, He was galvanized and ready for action in ministry.

If the root has no basis in the Word, as soon as it gets attacked, it'll get kicked out of the dirt, and it will not produce. So, if you really have a revelation, then you can know an attack will come that causes you to walk in the revelation, to galvanize what God is trying to do in your life.

Military boot-camp training is designed, in its premise, to teach and instill the counterbalance strategy. The counterbalance strategy is a military term meaning the ability to endure such a level of attack that you no longer focus on the attack, but on the response to it.

A lot of boot-camp coaches take the trainees away for days or weeks at a time and drill them intensely. What are they trying to do? They're trying to get them to break, because two things happen when people break: They either cry, or they fight and attack. The coaches are trying to push the trainees to that moment. Why? Because that's how they learn that they're stronger. They can endure more because they've pushed themselves to the limit.

Then the strategy for you is to have the ability to maintain the presence of mind and to detach yourself from all the chaos. Your ability to maintain your presence of mind in the midst of it all becomes an absolute strategy unto itself. Because if you can't keep your presence of mind, then you will no longer be able to hear what God is saying. You'll be too enamored with the attack in which you've found yourself.

Jesus was in the midst of the wilderness and all its inherent problems: the scarcity of food, the scarcity of shelter, the presence of vicious animals. He was in the midst of being totally engulfed by an attack, and then here comes Satan.

Some of you have never been through stuff like that, where things are happening in your life and you're like, "Oh my God, my job is all messed up, my kids are acting crazy." Then the car starts acting stupid and the refrigerator breaks, and then all of a sudden, as if that wasn't enough, here comes Satan with some old junk to try to throw into your life. And now you don't know which way is up, because you're focused on all that's going on around you.

You couldn't hear God if He walked into the room and screamed in your ear.

> **Ephesians 1:3-6**
> **Blessed be the God and Father of our Lord Jesus Christ, who hath blessed us with all spiritual blessings in heavenly places in Christ: According as he hath chosen us in him before the foundation of the world, that we should be holy and without blame before him in love: Having predestinated us unto the adoption of children by Jesus Christ to himself, according to the good pleasure of his will, To the praise of the glory of his grace, wherein he hath made us accepted in the beloved."**

PRINCIPLE 6: THE ART OF COUNTERBALANCE STRATEGY

A God who operates in eternity has already given you all spiritual blessing in eternity.

Because seasons are limited to time, they cannot affect your life. They cannot cause a different outcome; they can only influence it.

You need to understand that if you want to follow God, you'd better learn about seasons! Some of you get a word that was in season, but you move so slowly that the season has changed by the time you want to act. Then you blame God as if this *word* wasn't right, when it was *you* operating. If He's done it in eternity, then it must be revealed to you by the Spirit in time.

Just because you don't see it in time doesn't mean it hasn't already been done in eternity. The beautiful thing about God is that He doesn't have to *hide* something from you to hide it from you. He just has not to reveal it.

The challenge, though, is when God reveals it in time, He's not only revealing it to you, but He's revealing it to Satan. This is why you have to realize that in seasons come opportunity. If you have a problem with change, you will hold on to the last season, never realizing that the change of season is not negative. Seasons have to change! Can you imagine if it was 120 degrees every single day? Seasons and time bring opportunity, which is why you have to understand that God's omnipotence and omniscience give you some temporary power over your circumstances. But His are eternal.

That means He has knowledge and power over your time.

There are times when God will come into the season that you're in, and sometimes God will let the season rage. If God has revealed it in time or in eternity, then I've got to grab it in time. It becomes an element of my faith. I have to grab it in the realm of eternity because He does not live in time. Time changes your mind, not His.

Time only changes you because you can't wear God down. Because if a thousand years is like a blink to God, it doesn't matter how much you act in any way you want to act, it's still now to Him. When you've been begging God for something for 10 years? For God, it's still now. The measure of your faith is what you can bring from eternity now. God is not waiting to be a blessing to you. You're the one who has the limitation of time. Just try to manifest eternity.

As I go through situations in my life, I have to be mindful of the seasons. I experience time as it relates to my revelation of eternity. If I'm not careful, I'll become so consumed with the attack that my counterbalance strategy will be lost because I forget what I'm supposed to be doing in the midst of the battle. I'm out there fighting on the field, struggling for my life. And I lose sight of what has occurred in eternity because my circumstance has caused me to become so detached from the eternal that I begin succumbing in the natural. Now I'm tired, I'm exhausted, I'm worn out and I'm making bad decisions because all hell has broken loose against me. Then I'm struggling, because I don't understand that there are times and seasons for every single thing.

There's a season when you'll go through struggle, but guess what? Seasons have beginnings and ends, and as God takes you from one thing to the next, what He has set up in store for you eternally has not changed. It's already done. It's already handled. God is ready. Satan's goal in his art of war is to get you so distracted that you'll lose sight of eternity.

This is why they put you through so much in boot camp. They need you to be able to handle some things. They need you to be able to take a punch and not go, "I'm outta here! They didn't tell me these were *real* bullets!!"

Satan left Jesus for a more opportune time, because he knew that there would be other moments that were going to be more ideal for him. Later on, Jesus was sitting in the garden, the rest of His crew was falling asleep, and Satan said, "Oooh, here's a good time. Here's a good season."

People's whole lives go to hell, and *then* they want to find God. Church has been open every Sunday! They can come whenever they want to, and they don't. They're not consistent in any way, shape, or form. Then when all hell breaks loose in their life because the season has shifted, they don't know how to act in the season they're in because they missed their season of preparation!

PRINCIPLE 6: THE ART OF COUNTERBALANCE STRATEGY

You can't teach a man to swim while he's drowning. They didn't see the value of it until all hell broke loose. N*ow* they want to run to the altar crying, "Jesus, fix it!"

People don't realize that Satan's greatest attack comes in their ignorance. When you don't know the season you're in, he can wage an attack.

Satan was sitting there *waiting* for Jesus.

"Oh, He's going to the wilderness. Oh, look at that. He's out here in the middle of nowhere. Let me sit here and wait. Hey, dude's *got* to be hangry. Here's my opportunity!"

Seasons. He's waiting for moments of seasons, and when you're in the midst of one you'd better have a strategy that says, "I can endure this. I can get through this. Because I've been trained by the best, and this revelation will not pass! When I get into the middle of this situation, I am clear to count it all joy. I know I could *dance* my way out of this."

Satan is not omnipotent. He is not omnipresent. He is not omniscient, which means that he cannot be everywhere at the same time. He does not have all knowledge. He's not all powerful.

Only God can step out of eternity, step into your time, and give you everything you need for the time you're in.

Principle 7

THE ART *of* CORRESPONDING ACTION

FAITH WITHOUT ACTION IS THE SLOWEST ROUTE TO VICTORY. ACTION WITHOUT FAITH IS THE NOISE BEFORE DEFEAT.

James 2:14
What doth it profit, my brethren, though a man say he hath faith, and have not works? Can faith save him?

Faith without action is the slowest route to victory, and action without faith is the noise before defeat.

Faith without works is dead.

It is important to note here that James is not the only pastor, but he is the only *acting* pastor—he's the only one who wrote an epistle as an acting pastor. A lot of the disciples pastored at one point in time, but the epistle of James is the Bible's only epistle written by an *acting* pastor at that time. So the book of James is called "The Pastoral Epistle" because he is addressing pastoral topics, and it is "didactic," meaning it is instructional to you.

Some writings—Matthew, Mark, Luke, and John—are primarily historical. In other words, they tell you what happened and when it happened. They describe in detail the things that occurred biblically in ancient times. But James is didactic in the sense that it is telling you how to apply what occurred on Calvary. He makes it plain and simple so you can take Bible text or Bible understanding—what we have been afforded through Jesus' sacrifice for our lives—and learn how to apply that instruction in your life.

The challenge then becomes orthodox viewpoints, or orthodox belief.

Orthos means "correct." *Doxa* means "belief system."

Maybe you go to an orthopedic surgeon, or you get orthopedic inserts in your shoes. *Ortho* means "to correct" or "to right," and *Pedic* refers to your feet. *Orthodoxy* is the correct belief system, or the correct way of thinking and understanding.

One of the challenges in today's world is that the Orthodox belief system has been subverted for more of a reprobate mindset. This is the most biblically-illiterate generation we have ever seen. To be honest with you, I believe one of my main God-given goals and purposes for ministry is to deal with how illiterate reprobate people are concerning the Word of God. It is so important that you understand His Word so you can apply it to your life as the end days draw nearer.

The system at work within this world is, by nature, Babylonian. Whenever you see that Babylonian system come to its fruition and fullness, God says, "The iniquity is now full." In other words, "I've had enough of this nonsense."

God will allow things to happen in this world for a period of time.

People think God is just sitting back and allowing this nonsense, but that is not the case. God is allowing a span of time for people to get it right. What you confuse for apathy is really patience.

God is absolutely concerned with all the things that occur in this world, but He's allowing time for people to repent, to change, and to get it together. He's allowing time for the church to come up out of "Just Service" and realize that we have a greater responsibility beyond coming to the church and shouting unto the Lord. We have to stop just being *in* the church and start *being* the church. Because if you have noticed, if you have paid attention to what's going on in today's world, the world has crept into the church.

Many of these didactic, teaching epistles are designed to help you to learn how to apply what happened in your life when you received Jesus.

PRINCIPLE 7: THE ART OF CORRESPONDING ACTION

Some theologians believe that James wrote contradicting Paul, because Paul said that it is by faith and not works that you are saved. Here in verse 14, James wrote, "How can that type of faith save you?"

This looks like a problem between the two of them ... unless you recognize that Paul is not writing to believers. Paul is speaking to unbelievers—so he is talking about the *root* of salvation, while James is speaking to believers, about the *fruit* of our salvation.

From the very beginning of your life, you have an inability to follow God. You cannot understand God. You cannot follow God. You don't even like God. You don't even know God. You have started in a place where you are the complete antithesis of what would be considered godly.

So if I am God, how do I get you to a place where you are capable of receiving the object of your faith? Because, by your very nature, you could never handle what you keep asking for. So as you desire certain things, you have to realize that I (God) have to train you up through the process of patience to exercise your faith so that you're able to handle it.

A whole generation of Christians has come up believing they can accept Christ without forsaking the world. If you think you can accept Christ and not have to forsake the world, then you need to understand that's the complete opposite of what the Bible tells us. You are not functioning in the ways of God, you are functioning in the ways of the world—yet you act like a Jesus fan.

A fan is someone who likes something a whole lot, right? You might even be fanatical.

A fan shows up at a football game—483 pounds, half his body is painted blue, and the other half is painted white. He has no concern for how stupid he looks. Why? Because he's a fan of his team.

But the moment his team lets him down, he decides he no longer likes that team. So he paints his body half red and half black for the next game. He switches teams, which makes him a fan and not a follower. Even the demons are fans of God. They just don't do anything but tremble.

If I'm a follower of Jesus, then I submit to discipleship, which means discipline. It means that no matter what happens, no matter what the outcome—win or lose (and we know He always wins)—we are always following Him. We don't fit the church in around the football game. We don't fit the church in around the baseball game. I'm not a fan of God; I'm a follower of Christ. And as a follower, I'll follow Him into the depths of hell. I'll follow Him into heaven. I'll follow Him on earth, because I understand that when I follow, I don't decide what I *get* to do, but I do what I am *called* to do.

Some Christian folks will be like this:

Someone in need will say, "Hey, can I borrow $20?"

And they're like, "Oh, uh, well, let me just—I will pray for you! We'll believe God for it!"

Listen, if you have $20 in your pocket, quit being spiritual.

I'm quick to say, "Is that what you need?"

No, we're not going to pray about that. Why am I not praying about it? Because God has already provided it. If someone comes to me and says, "Pastor, I need $20," and I have $20 in my pocket, there's nothing for us to pray about.

Don't send people off and tell them, "Be warm and be fed. I'll pray for you." If you have the ability, then get it done, because you are the answer to someone else's problem.

The challenge is that most people walk around with a spirit of entitlement. They think everybody else is the answer to *their* problems, never realizing that *they* are the answer to *someone else's* problem. Wherever there is a need, there is a supply. They are magnetized to pull each other together. What you have will supply what someone else needs. When the Body of Christ comes together, no one in need should be sent off with "Just be warm!"

The antithesis to that is just because you have a need doesn't mean I have to respond to it.

PRINCIPLE 7: THE ART OF CORRESPONDING ACTION

In verses 14 through 18, James challenges Christians, "How could your faith help you if it has no action to it?"

If all you do is talk about how good God is, if all you do is walk around quoting scripture, you have Mental Assent. "Mental Assent" is where you have a mental understanding of scripture, but when your life comes under attack, even though you have knowledge in that area, you forsake knowledge for the attack!

"Yes, I know God can heal me, but the moment I get sick, I forget all about what God can do." That's Mental Assent. It means you have it in your *head*, but you really don't have it in your *heart*.

Our faith has to address the whole man, the whole person. You are made in God's image, which means you are three parts. You are a spirit, you live in a body, and you possess a soul. Your soul is your mind, your will, and your emotions. If our spirit is a spiritual thing, then how do we cause our body, our mind, will, and emotions—our soul—to line up with our faith? Genuine faith has a unification aspect of your spirit, soul, and body. Genuine faith has to be able to move your physical body, your soul (your mind, will, and emotions), and your spirit.

The challenge for most people is that they stop in the place of spiritual food because faith cometh by hearing the Word of God. Therefore, their spirit begins to grow, but they do not allow their mind to be renewed, which means their body can't move. God says that in order to move us from the place of iniquity and sin where we were conceived—to take us from faith to faith, from victory to victory, from glory to glory—He has to allow us to get into some situations that will cause our faith to be tried by fire, to produce a genuineness out of it. Otherwise, we'll never get into faith beyond just our head.

> **James 2:19-20**
> **Thou believest that there is one God; thou doest well: the devils also believe, and tremble. But wilt thou know, O vain man, that faith without works is dead?**

They don't allow what they know God to be to influence their will and change their behavior. They do know that God is, but they don't know anything else about how to allow God to lead their lives.

Our worldview tends to be a reflection of our faith. How we view the world gives a clear indication of how we view God. In other words, what we receive from God is directly related to how we see Him. Because our experience with God is idiosyncratic to us as individuals, we have to be careful of what knowledge we allow to develop in our soul (mind, will, and emotions). We must purposefully develop and pursue a greater understanding of spiritual things. Our faith must always be reaching beyond where we currently are, pulling us into the greater that God has in store.

As it reaches the impossible, our faith has to stretch. You don't borrow money from a homeless person. And when you come to God, you have to believe that He is greater than you are.

Faith has to have a psychological effect. As faith forms my worldview, it becomes of utmost importance that I guard my life against that which seeks to impede my progress. If my worldview is framed by my exposure, then fear can cause not my *spirit* but my *mind* to change regarding the object of my affection. That can move me from a fan to a follower, or from a follower to a fan.

As Christians, we're challenged if we begin to introduce psychology, because people are so vehemently against it. They say, "Psychology has nothing to do with God!"

That is not true. We have to change the way we think about something in order to act a certain way; and our worldview determines how we act.

People say, "You should have done such-and-such with your money because there are starving people in the world!" That's like telling your child, "You need to eat all the food on your plate because there are starving kids in Africa!"

PRINCIPLE 7: THE ART OF CORRESPONDING ACTION

What a person does with the money that God has given them responsibility for is between them and God. There's always a one-talent Christian who wants to tell a five-talent Christian how to do things.

If your faith calls you beyond your comfort zone, you will criticize what you ought to be believing God for because you can't seem to get there from where you're living.

James, as a pastor trying to get people to walk in the fullness of God, tells you that the success of your faith is tied to your faith's ability to produce. Otherwise, your faith is vanity. You can give God all the glory, but James says if you have no faith, it's impossible to please God. This is why his message is didactic. He's telling you this is how you do it. He says to move out of vanity and allow your faith to produce something in you.

> **James 2:14-22**
> **What doth it profit, my brethren, though a man say he hath faith, and have not works? can faith save him? If a brother or sister be naked, and destitute of daily food, And one of you say unto them, Depart in peace, be ye warmed and filled; notwithstanding ye give them not those things which are needful to the body; what doth it profit? Even so faith, if it hath not works, is dead, being alone. Yea, a man may say, Thou hast faith, and I have works: shew me thy faith without thy works, and I will shew thee my faith by my works. Thou believest that there is one God; thou doest well: the devils also believe, and tremble. But wilt thou know, O vain man, that faith without works is dead? Was not Abraham our father justified by works, when he had offered Isaac his son upon the altar? Seest thou how faith wrought with his works, and by works was faith made perfect?**

In verse 22, he's talking about Abraham, and how Abraham offered up Isaac on the altar. He says that his faith was cooperating with his actions and that by his actions, his faith was perfected or made mature.

The church has rejected the concept of psychology in lieu of religion.

The church says, "If you've got problems, Jesus is what gets you healed!"

Then the health care profession says, "Stay away from religion" Many healthcare professionals will tell you not to preach to people who struggle with mental illness because it adds a dimension of problems they can't sort through.

The church says mental healthcare is not necessary, and the mental healthcare industry says the church is not necessary. Yet there's not a prison in America that does not promote scripture, Bible, and religion. Why? Because they know that religion is the ultimate tamer of that which is attainable.

Doctors, faith, and medicine work together. Luke was a physician. There's nothing wrong with medicine. There's nothing wrong with understanding psychology as it relates to your Christianity.

I've spent some time in mental wards. Believe it or not, some people who have been classified as mentally insane can quote scripture better than a lot of church people. And I largely believe that many who are called end up in prison or in mental wards because their worldview has never been framed properly to understand the dilemma that is innate in the call of God.

God certainly transcends psychology. In other words, He is eternal, omnipotent, omnipresent, omniscient. He is beyond psychology. Yet the problem is that you have to process Him through your psychology—through your mind, will, and emotions—to get to know the fullness of who He is.

Faith without corresponding action is like a profession with no practice.

It's like a doctor who says, "I'm a doctor!"

"Oh? Where's your office?"

"I don't have one."

If you are believing God for your healing, but every time you get sick, you stay home from work, you stay home from church, is it altering your life? Then your behavior corresponds to the problem and not to your faith. If our action is supposed to correspond to our belief, then we must always

PRINCIPLE 7: THE ART OF CORRESPONDING ACTION

check what we're doing against what we're believing. If I'm believing God for a new car, it's not going to show up at my house. I have to go out and look at dealerships and have conversations to allow God the ability to move in the situation. If I don't go out there in some way, shape, or form, it will never happen. Faith without action is the slowest route to victory.

> **Luke 5:1-4**
> **And it came to pass, that, as the people pressed upon him to hear the word of God, he stood by the lake of Gennesaret, And saw two ships standing by the lake: but the fishermen were gone out of them, and were washing their nets. And he entered into one of the ships, which was Simon's, and prayed him that he would thrust out a little from the land. And he sat down, and taught the people out of the ship. Now when he had left speaking, he said unto Simon, Launch out into the deep, and let down your nets for a draught.**

Do you translate action as faith?

People say things like, "I've been tithing all this time, and nothing seems to be working!"

Then you're not talking about faith. If you keep *saying* that nothing's working, then nothing's working. You have what it is you have hooked your faith to. So what you really have is what your corresponding action produces. Whatever your actions are tied to, that's what your faith produces.

If your fear forces your action, you get a bad report from the doctor. The doctor says you're not going to live. You get into fear. You then come after God's heart, but you did it out of fear, not out of faith. Your corresponding action was fear.

So it is not the faith that determines your outcome; it's the corresponding action working in partnership with your faith that produces the outcome.

> **Luke 5:5-7**
> **And Simon answering said unto him, Master, we have toiled all the night, and have taken nothing: nevertheless at thy word I will let down the net. And when they had this done, they inclosed a great multitude of fishes: and their net brake.**

> And they beckoned unto their partners, which were in the other ship, that they should come and help them. And they came, and filled both the ships, so that they began to sink.

These are not amateurs. They are professional fishermen who have been out fishing all night. Jesus says, "Let me use your boat to preach the gospel."

He preaches the gospel. They think He's going ashore, but He turns around and says, "You were so nice to me, here's what I'm going to do. Go out there on your boat, drop your net, and you'll bring in a huge catch."

Simon Peter is a professional fisherman. He's used to catching fish. Do you have *any idea* the size of the catch that caused this man who *does this for a living* to see how his boat is sinking?

> **Luke 5:9**
> **For he was astonished, and all that were with him, at the draught of the fishes which they had taken.**

This is the biggest catch he has ever made in his entire life. This is the coup de gras. This is the moment that every fisherman begs for. This great catch has almost sunk his boat, and he says, "I am not a fan of Jesus—I'm a *follower*."

> **Luke 5:10**
> **And so was also James, and John, the sons of Zebedee, which were partners with Simon. And Jesus said unto Simon, Fear not; from henceforth thou shalt catch men.**

Jesus said, "Today, you just know how to fish. But my purpose in you has created extension because now you'll be fishers of men. I'll expand you because you did what I told you."

Many people want extension to follow disobedience. They want more without having done the corresponding action. They will never see extension, and if they're not careful, they'll become even more

PRINCIPLE 7: THE ART OF CORRESPONDING ACTION

disappointed, because people don't see extension when they haven't mastered expansion.

This is the place where Satan wages his greatest attack, because he knows that if he can move you into complacency, you will never act. If he can keep you apathetic, you will never act. You'll just talk about how much faith you have. When it comes time to exercise it? You give like a pauper instead of like the wealthy person you aspire to be. You allow sickness to rule your life instead of functioning as a healthy person would function. You make yourself feel better by associating with people whose levels of revelation are lower than yours instead of seeking out those who already have greater levels of revelation and saying, "I want to come up."

You must not be afraid to allow yourself to be around people who will cause you to reach. But when you reach, you'd better have action corresponding to your reach and not to your fear. Your level of manifestation will always fall to the level of your proclivity. So you've got to learn that if you want to do battle, you have to stretch. And as you stretch, the corresponding action has to go with the stretch. And that means you've got to be around people who know how to act at that level.

PRINCIPLE 8

THE ART *of* LAYING PLANS
HAVING THE RIGHT PLAN LEADS TO VICTORY. BRUTE STRENGTH IS NOT ENOUGH..

Having the right plan leads to victory, because brute strength is not enough.

It is extremely important for you to understand God's plan for your life, and to discern the season God has you in and why you're there.

I've watched people make decisions, completely disregarding God's plan for their lives. They will move across the country, they will find themselves in places because of a job transfer or for ungodly reasons. They put themselves in positions following things that are not God's plan.

Just because you don't understand it doesn't mean it's not God's plan for your life!

> **Psalm 127:1-3**
> **Except the Lord build the house, they labour in vain that build it: except the Lord keep the city, the watchman waketh but in vain. It is vain for you to rise up early, to sit up late, to eat the bread of sorrows: for so he giveth his beloved sleep. Lo, children are an heritage of the Lord: and the fruit of the womb is his reward.**

If the Lord is going to build the house, why do *we* have to build the house?

And what in the world is the "house" that we're talking about? He's not talking about a physical house. If he was, what do children have to do with that? What he means by "house" here is like "The House of David," referring not only to David, but also to David's children, David's children's children, and all their descendants. "The House of" refers to the system related to all that pertains to you.

If I have to labor to build something that God has already built, what is the point of both of us constructing the very same thing?

He says that you don't have to stay up late, and you don't have to work 10 jobs. You don't have to sacrifice your Sundays and Wednesdays in order to try to make extra money to buy the things you need to have. God can bless you in your faithfulness to that which He's called you to.

There is no question, there are no ifs, ands, or buts about it. There is nothing more important than the call and the plan of God for our lives. The truth then becomes that we're all, in fact, building a system or a house in our lives.

Whether you know it or not, you are building a system in your home. You are teaching your kids certain things that you think they're not paying attention to when they are actually watching you very closely. You pick on their traits and characteristics when the truth of the matter is that they got them from you! That is the system you built, whether you did it unwittingly or you did it on purpose. You can build a system that will create a poverty mindset for *generations* because of how *you* think. You have affected your children.

Many people criticize a prosperous person instead of rejoicing with them. That poverty-minded attitude rubs off on their kids who adapt the same critical stance toward prosperity. Instead of teaching our kids that prospering is not everything, we need to help them understand its valid importance—right up there with oxygen. While true biblical prosperity is not limited to money, it does include money. So when some silly-behind boy wants to take your daughter out on a date to a fast-food joint, your daughters should have better taste or a better palette or a higher opinion of herself than that! It starts with you creating a higher standard of expectation.

PRINCIPLE 7: THE ART OF LAYING PLANS

Too many Christians think standards don't matter. I believe they do. If a boy's idea of a quality date for your daughter is to take her back to his house to "Netflix and chill," your children should have a higher standard than to settle for such a cheap date. If their idea of a fancy date is some fast food joint, that's tragic. Our children ought to have better expectations for themselves than that.

As you establish a higher standard and system, the system begins retraining people in how to think. As people think differently and adopt higher standards, they will function differently.

So if God is building the house, you are building the house. Yet you still have to labor to build it? God, as the Chief Architect, has built it in the Spirit, so it is purely the blueprint for what you are supposed to construct in your life. If your house exists in the blueprint, then where is it? It's in the realm of the Spirit

The nature of altruism is the idea "I will sacrifice myself for your benefit."

Let's say, for example, that somebody gets a new home. People might say, "Why couldn't you have gotten a smaller home? Hmm? Why'd you have to get one that's so big?"

The altruistic thought process says he should sacrifice himself for the greater common good of everyone else. Right? The problem is that it's narcissistic, because if he has to diminish his demand in order to meet yours, then it is not God. It becomes narcissistic for him to think in an altruistic way, to say "I'll sacrifice me so that you can have," because now God cannot sacrifice!

Can God even sacrifice anyway? If someone decides to build a $50 million house and God provides the money for it, does God have to go to His banker and say, "I'm going to need to borrow $50,000,000?"

If all the silver and gold in the world belong to Him, then it's no big deal to meet your need. Someone once told me that if you have to act like you're not prospering in order to keep people happy, it's like you being healthy and pretending to be sick because you don't want other sick people to be sad.

Whose plan are you following? The world's definition of happiness is defined by a mood, but the *real* definition of happiness is "a state of wellbeing that encompasses living a good life with meaning and deep satisfaction."

> **Ephesians 2:10**
> **For we are his workmanship, created in Christ Jesus unto good works, which God hath before ordained that we should walk in them.**

You mean to tell me that if I want to live the good life, then all I have to know is the plan that was predestined—or planned beforehand—and follow it? I don't need 10 jobs?

If happiness is the final state of wellbeing that encompasses living a good life with meaning and deep satisfaction, then happiness is not relegated to having more possessions—it's really relegated to purpose.

If you let people sway your mood, then they can control your happiness—if that's what you believe real happiness is. So as my mood changes, I can allow my emotions to reign over my happiness.

People say, "I'm looking for a soulmate." You don't want a soulmate; your soul is jacked up! You do not want anyone to recognize and to connect to your soul in a relational way, because your soul is a mess! Your soul encompasses your mind, your will, and your emotions. If you're an emotional wreck, you don't want a soulmate.

So if true happiness is based on satisfaction and in accordance with perceived purpose, then one of the enemy's greatest weapons against you in his warfare is to cause you to become discontent and sway your emotions. If he can sway your emotions, then he can move you out of God's best plan for you.

Scientific experiments always include a "control." A control is a standard; it doesn't change throughout the course of the experiment. Then the scientist can adjust other things, "variables," and they can see how the variables affect the control. If the control changes *and* the variables

PRINCIPLE 7: THE ART OF LAYING PLANS

change, there's no way for me to assess the experiment to find out what is really causing the problem, because everything keeps changing!

It's like a computer, or like our church's sound system. You have to isolate different possible causes for a problem until you pinpoint the one thing that is actually the problem, and that's the variable.

You've got to have a control. You'll never know whether or not you are successful in life if what you base your life on is not a control, but a variable.

Satan tries to get you to think that everything is situational. The nature of variables causes you to live your life in the benchmark of what is not consistent and solid. So when you come to church, our whole purpose is to keep getting it into you that *this* is God's plan. It does not change. God's Word is unchanging. This is the Word by which we live. We don't let it go up and down and all around because then you'll never know where you hit against the mark.

That's why Paul said, "I press towards the mark of the high calling of God." The high calling is higher than anything that you could ever imagine. Therefore, what you benchmark your life towards is the high calling, and it's always pulling you higher up and deeper in.

Satan comes in and says, "No, it's not that serious; trust me! If God had really meant it that way? Come on, Eve—just take a bite."

One of the first true signs that you are out of God's will is an absolute discontentment with your life. Because if God gives you a plan and you're following the plan, you come in with a whole different opportunity. If I know God's plan for my life, then I am not swayed by what other people will do or say, because I know what God's plan is.

When I benchmark my life, I benchmark it against the plan of God for my life.

If the plan or the standard is above where I'm living, then I know I have to come up. If I am already moving toward where I'm supposed to go, you can't disappoint me, because my disappointment is not vested in your feelings. My satisfaction is based on knowing the plan of God, knowing the will of God, and functioning from that place. So no matter what you say or what you come up with, I am not moved by your opinion! But to do that, you have to be rooted in truth, because if you want everybody to like you, you chose the wrong faith.

The house you are building is not just a house. It's not a physical structure —it's a system. It's everything concerning your life. You have to have God's plan, you have to know God's plan, and you have to follow God's plan.

I've heard people say, "I just feel like I've got to move." OK, what did *God* say?

"Nothing." OK then, you know what you're supposed to do—sit down and shut up.

Take several seats and let Him run, because you might be in the place that's just before He moves in your life, and you don't even know it! He knows the end from the beginning, and the beginning from the end.

After Jesus was crucified then resurrected, but He hadn't ascended yet, He was sitting on the beach cooking some fish. The rest of the crew had gone back to being fishermen. They spotted Him, conversation ensued, but here's the point: They had just been with Jesus for *three years*. They'd seen miracle after miracle. He told them what he wanted them to do. He trained them to do what He'd called them to do, and the first thing they did was go back to being *fishermen*.

The fastest way to steal a person's vision is to give him another one.

That's why if you're not careful, you'll compare yourself to somebody else. You'll look at someone and say, "He's a businessman, so I'm going to be a businessman!"

You're never going to be a businessman if you can't delay your reward, because every business person knows you don't get instant gratification. You are sowing and planting and changing diapers and burping that thing,

PRINCIPLE 7: THE ART OF LAYING PLANS

and it's crapping all over the place, and you have to attend to it when there's not a nickel coming in!

People get funny when they think, "Oh, you're a businessman. I want to be a businessman like you!"

If you ain't willing to work, don't do it. If you wouldn't take a job in a pie factory eating pies, knock it off. You're better off going to work for somebody else and letting them pay you to do absolutely nothing.

The nature of what you want to be can come by *comparison* instead of by *leading*.

"Well, I see so-and-so is this; I can do that! I'm smarter than they are!" *Are you?*

Many people have looked back at their life and were mad at what they built, because what they built was not what they wanted. They're disappointed, they're like "This is not what my life was supposed to be. This is not what I envisioned. I had dreams. I had hopes. I could've been a contender!"

As you reflect on the system you've built, remember God tries to tell you ahead of time that it's vain, that it produces nothing to build a system that He did not build.

He says, "If *you* build it, it doesn't matter how much effort you put into it, it will never produce what you want from it. You can get up early, you can stay up late, you can work all kinds of days and times, but unless I am the one protecting the house, unless I am the one who is guarding this thing, unless I am the one who constructed this thing in the Spirit, it doesn't matter what you do in the natural, you will never keep it—because I give to my beloved even in sleep."

> **Romans 8:28**
> **And we know that all things work together for good to them that love God, to them who are the called according to his purpose.**

THE ART OF WAR

The first thing Sun Tzu talks about in *The Art of War* is the art of laying plans. He says brute strength is not enough; having the right plan guarantees victory.

Are tired of struggling? Do you want to have some victory? If you want guaranteed victory, then you've got to know God's plan.

> **Jeremiah 17:9**
> **The heart is deceitful above all things, and desperately wicked: who can know it?**

When God asks you a question, He's really letting you know something that you need to know, something that you evidently don't.

This is where you get into people saying, "My heart wants what He wants." Your heart is desperately wicked. Tell it to shut up.

Girl meets boy. Boy is a good boy—respectful, honorable, doing what he has to do. He loves the Lord. She thinks he's boring. She wants a bad boy because she needs a project.

"I can change him!"

He doesn't go to church. Ain't worth a wooden nickel. He plays video games all day. Ain't got no job. You're working your tail feather off to take care of him, to give him the milk when he should've bought the cow. But he's a bad boy. And the good boy, the one who sits a few rows away from you in church, he's too goody-two-shoes for you.

You think narcissistically that you are greater than God, so you think that somehow you could throw him in church and turn it all into sunshine. God couldn't change him, but you, all of a sudden, certainly can!

Next thing you know, you're complaining because you're in a life that you didn't want to be in with a person you shouldn't have been with, while the good guy has found himself someone else because he was willing to stay with the plan of God, and God brought him the right person.

You're constantly complaining, "Girl, he just ain't no good."

PRINCIPLE 7: THE ART OF LAYING PLANS

He wasn't no good when you met him!

"I don't know what I'm gonna do, my heart just wants what it wants!"

Tell your heart to shut up, because your heart is desperately wicked and is trying to mess with the plan of God.

Tennis rackets have what they call the "sweet spot," which is the portion of the racket that produces the maximum effect with the least amount of effort. If you are skilled at hitting the sweet spot, you don't have to hit the ball as hard, right?

In your sweet spot, you don't have to work as hard to build a life. If you're in the sweet spot, the only time you have to exert an immense amount of energy to try to make it fit is when you're trying to jam a square peg into a round hole. It's when you are trying to figure how to force what God did not build into your life—and now you want Him to bless *your* plan, when your plan was not *His* plan. Now you're exerting all of this effort, you're tired, you're worn out while there are other people who are just rolling through it.

Life is good. God is good.

Are you working so hard because you don't know your sweet spot? Because the sweet spot is God. That's the place with the least amount of effort, where you can actually work with God and begin to realize that you don't have to stay "Just Satisfied." You just have to submit to His plan.

When you submit to His plan, you stop looking for adventure. You're out looking for your husband at the age of 20, when you should be looking for your husband with the mindset of 40. The adventure gets old when y'all have kids and he's still trying to go to the club!

You single guys, you come to church and you're like "I want a good church girl," but you're out looking for ladies in the club! Then you say, "Well, what's wrong with so-and-so? She doesn't make me wait until we get married!" Oh, OK. So let me see if I understand this correctly: You want to go to the club and find one who won't make you wait. But she won't make your friend (and his friend, and his friend's friend) wait, either.

When it comes to seeing their worldview, most people have a problem with not allowing God's view to become their view. Because if they saw God's view, they would have a different understanding of what's going on in the world.

Most people are not self-deprecating. Most people are not self-loathing. So for you to admit that your *heart* is wicked means having to admit that *you* are wicked.

If your heart is wicked, you'd better be careful what you allow your heart to drive you into.

"Well, you just don't understand, Pastor, I can't help myself!" No—you can. When you begin to see God's plan and how God wants you to do it, you will handle things differently.

I'm very careful. I don't allow people who have low revelation to be close to me.

I've had people try to reach out to me and my wife. "Come on, Pastor, can we go do this? Can we go skating? Can we go do this or that?" No, because you have low revelation and don't know the plan of God. If you get too close to me, Satan can start whispering to me. That means you are my enemy, and I let you in in the first place.

If you're honest about some of the people that have betrayed you, you'll see: You let them in. That's how they got access to get close enough to you.

Some of you married somebody who will always betray you. Some of you are dating someone who is always betraying you. Some of you have best friends who have always betrayed you. Here you are, wondering how they got in so close to you, and you are *so angry*, never having realized that you did not deny them access.

PRINCIPLE 7: THE ART OF LAYING PLANS

did. They might have used their own sword, but it was God who made all their enemies fall! It was God, with an outstretched arm, who put them in the spot they were in to get the opportunity they got to bless their life and take them where they wanted to go.It was God.

"Pastor, you don't understand! I've been through so much, and if God really was there, how could He let me go through the things that I went through? That woman molested me. That man raped me. You don't understand the stuff I had to fight through. The person who was supposed to protect and take care of me did things to me. How could God allow that thing to happen?"

God was in the room when it happened. He sees the end from the beginning and the beginning from the end. You need to learn from what you've been through, because God is going to take that thing and do something with it. It would have killed somebody else. He couldn't have let it happen to somebody else. It happened to you because He knew that one day, you'd be strong enough to walk it out in this life.

He was there in the moment when it went down. He knew.

You have to go through some stuff. It's good for you to have been afflicted.

But from a narcissistic standpoint, we have decided that we want to dictate the route.

Think about it this way: Difficulties and challenges in our life breed suspicion. Mama goes and buys a car, and she has a very bad experience. So she walks into the next car dealership she goes to with a chip on her shoulder. Adversity has now rerouted expectation.

Here's another example: A young lady is dating a guy. He does her really wrong, so she finally breaks free from that. She gets loose from all of that, and now she meets the good guy, the one God planned for. She says, "I don't need no man; God's got me!" Adversity reroutes expectation.

If you're not careful, you will have the plan, but adversity will come and redirect the plan because you listened to the negative voice. As you careen through life, quit letting bumps along the way redirect your expectation because you're mad about the guy who left you—especially while you're married to the guy who stayed! You're struggling with what So-and-so did to you 20 years ago while you are married to a man who loves you unconditionally.

Satan has thrown roadblocks that sway your expectations, so you become bitter and not better. And now your expectations are so low even a cricket could jump over them.

Freedom comes when the things you're ashamed of no longer bind you, when you allow what was used as a weapon against you to be forged into your armor to protect you. You need to allow everything Satan meant for a weapon to become galvanized because it brings you into relationship with God.

I don't care how many swords you've got. I don't care how many guns you've got. I don't care how smart you are. I don't care how pretty you think you are. I don't care how tall you are. I don't care how short you are. I don't care how gifted you are. I don't care how talented you are. I don't care if you got more degrees than a thermometer. There's no way you could have kept me down!

God needs a remnant of people who are willing to stand up and say, "I will fight for the plan of God. I don't care if it doesn't feel good. I don't care if it doesn't look a certain way. I will live in God's perfect plan and watch how He will bless me. Watch how God will move on my behalf while you're struggling. I ain't moving because of a job. I'm not moving because of stuff. I'm not disconnected because He's not saying what I want to hear. I know the plan, I know the will, I'm in the middle of it, and I'm staying right here because this is a sweet spot. This is where I get the most results."

Principle 9

THE ART *of* UNITY

A WINNING ARMY MUST BE UNITED BY THE SAME SPIRIT THROUGHOUT ALL ITS RANKS.

I saved the best principle of *The Art of War* for last. And I think it's one of the most important: A winning army must be united by the same Spirit throughout all its ranks. The Art of Unity is so significant, and I think it is one of the things that is probably fought for the hardest because Satan knows it is much easier to conquer those he can divide.

> **Luke 11:14**
> **And he was casting out a devil, and it was dumb. And it came to pass, when the devil was gone out, the dumb spake; and the people wondered.**

You will always have haters. If you don't have any haters, you're not doing anything, because haters are truly the breakfast of champions! If you are doing anything significant, you will always have to deal with them.

People are, by nature, judgmental. They have thoughts about you that don't pertain to who you really are. In some ways, they may be jealous and envious. And let me explain to you, there's a difference between jealousy and envy. You have to be clear as to which you mean. Jealousy and envy are not the same things.

Let's say a man sees that another man has a new car. He might be *envious* of their new car. But let's say the new car owner calls the man's wife and says, "Hey, I want to take you for a ride in my new car!"

So she gets in the new car with the man who's not her husband and goes for a ride. Her husband might now be *jealous* because what is his has been used by somebody else. In other words, you cannot be jealous of what you don't have. So jealousy comes into play when *his* wife is involved. Envy is dealing with things that don't belong to you; jealousy is dealing with things that do belong to you that are being shared or enjoyed by somebody else.

Remember that altruism says, "I will subject myself to whatever it is you need at the expense of myself." In other words, "I will sacrifice *me* to bless *you*." The problem with altruism is that although it sounds noble from a worldly perspective, it's absolutely demonic.

If I have to decrease in order for you to increase, it's not God.

Now, that does not mean that we do not use our resources to bless people, that we do not use what we have to be a blessing to others. That's not what I'm saying.

Here's an example. People run into financial problems and they get 10 jobs. Now they're working all day every day. They stop going to their church. Then when all hell breaks loose, that's when they want to run back to their church.

They should've learned how to swim when they were in swimming lessons, if you know what I mean. But because the job was more important, they moved, they left, they did whatever the job required them to do. They worked on Sundays. They no longer showed up at church. Then they figured out that they have to work harder to have more. Now their family suffers. Now the kids don't see them anymore. Now they're talking about their new car, how God has blessed them. God didn't bless them with that! Their kids should not have to suffer growing up with an absentee dad!

If I have a supply, and God is, in fact, God, then He does not need me to make whatever He's going to make happen. I don't have to take away from anything in order for Him to function. He doesn't need my child to suffer in order for Him to be God. He is God all by himself!

If I have to give up everything in my life, what does it matter?

PRINCIPLE 9: THE ART OF UNITY

If I can preach the paint off the walls, but I am not a husband to my wife?

A lot of ministers get caught up in that mindset. That's why their kids are off the chain.

"I'm serving God," they say. No, you've got to serve your family, because if you have to serve God at the *expense* of your family, you are not operating under an anointing!

Unfortunately, the altruistic thought process influences many people to think that practicing selfless concern makes them selfless. But do you see how self-centered this type of thinking actually is in terms of unity? Where does God come into the picture when you are the one paying out of your own idea of selflessness? This is the challenge as it relates to becoming unified in everything we do, because two thoughts come along with the idea that I'm going to get along with you.

The first one is that I have to decrease—or that I have to let go of or abandon what I want in order to get along with you. I've got to get rid of *me* to be with *you*. This is a problem with relationships as they begin to bud because of the attraction and the lust and the infatuation. People are often willing to jettison *you* to be with someone else. Because the ideology of being in love—of being in a relationship—far exceeds the reality of who *you* have become.

So what you typically do is introduce your potential suitor to a representative of *you* , but it is not really *you* because you have put aside all the things that really make you, *You*! And then there comes the point at which you have denied self for so long that you become angry about it. You become disappointed about it. Hope deferred makes the heart sick, but when it comes, it's like a tree of life. So you have been deferred for so long that now you want what *you* want, and you come to the realization that it clashes with what *they* want. So now you have the struggle, the battle trying to figure out "What do I do? Do I have to lose *me* to find *you*?"

The other side of this altruism is in order to be in unity or to present a unified front, I'll have to do something illegal or immoral. And if I object to it and you tell me I've got to go along anyway, then you are forcing me to go against the fabric of my beliefs.

Now, I can take the moral high ground and get that righteous indignation: "How dare you try to get me to go against what I believe!"

Never mind the fact that what *you* believe could be wrong.

> **Luke 11:14**
> **And he was casting out a devil, and it was dumb. And it came to pass, when the devil was gone out, the dumb spake; and the people wondered.**

Now, "dumb" doesn't mean stupid, as we use the word today—"dumb" meant that a person couldn't speak. Notice that the person's *attributes* were directly tied to the attributes of the spirit. The spirit was dumb; the person was dumb. We see this in many places. The spirit is sick; the person is sick. Largely, people fail to understand that many things that attack our physical bodies or move in our lives are not necessarily natural. They are quite spiritual.

So here comes Jesus, and He casts out this devil. And people say, "You are casting out devils through the spirit of Beelzebub," which is "the lord of the flies."

They're attributing deliverance to demonic activity.

Jesus never responds directly to the crowd's accusations and misrepresentations of His works.

He says to them, "If I cast out devils by a devil, then who do your children do it by? Who do *you* cast out devils with? If I'm doing it with the devil, then *you* must be doing it with the devil."

It doesn't even make any sense. And notice what He says: A kingdom divided against itself shall not stand. He's not talking about the Kingdom of God, He's talking about *Satan's* kingdom.

In other words, He's saying that Satan's kingdom is not divided.

PRINCIPLE 9: THE ART OF UNITY

In 1857, the U.S. Supreme Court ruled in the Dred Scott case, allowing Southern slave owners to take slaves into the Western territories, where slavery was illegal and Dred Scott had lived as a free man for two years. In 1858, Abraham Lincoln gave a speech called "A House Divided" before Congress—and it was unique, because he led with the "house divided" scripture.

Many people believe that Abraham Lincoln was the freer of slaves, so to speak; that that was his core cause, and he championed the cause, and they allot a great amount of regard to him because they believe he was the one who created the ideology or the reasoning behind why slaves should be free.

But in this House Divided speech, Lincoln didn't say there should be no slaves. What he said was, *either we all have slaves or none have slaves*—in other words, either the *entire country* has to accept slavery, or we've got to abolish slavery. But he said keeping us betwixt two positions is going to kill us and destroy us. His point wasn't the moral, ethical, or spiritual implications of slavery. It was the fact that division was present, and it would destroy the entire country if the states didn't get on the same page. And the truth of the matter is that he didn't care which page.

The nature of getting along, so to speak, is what breeds all these different types of ministries.

Do I believe there are times where you have to have men's meetings and women's meetings?

Yes, I do.

But have you noticed that there's almost an overwhelming reliance upon the separation of genders when it comes to spiritual meetings? It almost implies that the same word that is preached to the men cannot be preached effectively to the women. And if you want my honest opinion, I think it goes too far because I don't need to have 10 women's conferences in order to articulate to you as a woman what the Bible is saying to you. Because there is no difference, right? There is no difference. Both men and women are spiritual beings.

The perception, then, is that I have to be like you in order to be in unity with you. And the problem is that, while it's true in some situations, it's not true in all situations. Because then there's a unity of diversity—and unity of diversity is best represented in music.

We have horns, we got drums, we've got a piano, we've got a bass guitar and an electric guitar, and everybody plays together. If we are playing our parts on the same song, you hear music. If everyone is playing a different song, you hear noise. The difference between noise and music is whether or not we're in sync with each other. We are playing harmonies so there is diversity, yet there is unity.

There's also the unity of submission, capitulating for the greater common good. And as you submit, you have to realize that you cannot submit until you have submitted to something that you deem less than you.

I'll give it to you a different way: You can't be in jail and say, "I submitted to the cops."

You don't have a choice!

That's how the spirit of Jezebel works. It'll get into a church, work in a ministry, and here's what'll happen. People will be under a particular leader—let's say a worship leader.

The worship leader tells them, "I want you to pick up that bucket and move it from there to there."

A spirit of Jezebel will reject the leader's direction.

"Why do I have to do that? Why can't somebody else do it? Why? When does it need to get there? Well, what makes you qualified?"

Then the pastor comes along and tells the same person, "I need you to move that bucket from there to there." And they grab it and move it.

The Jezebel spirit has an inability to be unified what they deem laterally, so they're always critical of the leader's skill set. They always question their qualifications: "Is she smart enough? Is she good enough? Does she have enough excellence? Does she have enough?" They always have

PRINCIPLE 9: THE ART OF UNITY

resistance unilaterally because they deem themselves higher than the leader. But when a person of greater authority walks into the room, they know they've got to submit. So they're not submitting out of submission. They are submitting because they know they are in the presence of a greater authority, which makes it not submission, but acquiescence.

The only way I can submit to you is if I deem myself possibly greater than you and still lower myself to say, "Tell me what you want me to do."

Now I can bring unity by my submission because I don't think so highly of myself. Because I can step back and say, "If you want to do it that way, let's do it that way."

We're faced with the challenge that haters really shouldn't hate. Ultimately you need to realize that the gift that's in someone else is actually there for you. There is no possible way to be broke with unity. Do you see that when there's true unity, what I have, you have! When you're struggling, I'm able to take on your burden because we're in unity. Because we're in unity, I can help you even when you can't help yourself. The very person you envy has the ability to bless you because we need each other. The gift that is in you is something I need, because we are the Body! There is something in you that God has placed there to meet someone else's need.

This is why we are the Body. If you could do it on your own, you'd have done it already.

The people who are the most divisive struggle constantly. Why? Because they're not unified.

"I don't want to help somebody I don't like."

You're going to talk trash about me, do all kinds of stupid things to sow division, and then when you struggle and come to me, you wonder why I ain't jumping? Unity brings a place of connection that you can't lack when you're unified. There's no reason for hating!

If God loved me more than He loved you? I wish He did, but He does not. I like to think I'm His favorite child. I really do. I like to think that if God had a refrigerator, my picture would be on it!

But He doesn't.

Divisive people have a critical spirit and are always looking for other people's weaknesses. You can always tell someone who's divisive, because the majority of their conversation is related to a person's weakness. Every time they say something, they're talking negatively about somebody's inability to be as great as they are. They look for those things.

Some people have become so contrarian that they think it's cute. Everybody else is going this way, and you've got one of these kids who says, "I just have to be different! I'm not going to go along with the crowd because I'm special. I'm different."

It's narcissism. Division is always rooted in competitiveness.

Competitiveness looks for weaknesses, then focuses on them to exploit them for the win.

Why do coaches and their players watch tapes and footage of games before they go play a game? Why do they sit around in the training room and watch footage of their opponents?

Because they are looking to exploit weaknesses.

You are not supposed to be in competition with one another in the Body of Christ.

You are supposed to say, "Let me find your strength, and let me bring my strength and together we can do more than we could've done before." Because the truth of the matter is it is not possible to not share my blessing with you! If I have, you have. If you've got, I've got. We come to a place in unity where we're able to say we are each contributing.

Now, it's funny how contribution works—any relationship without reciprocity will die.

In other words, if you're a taker, you'll kill your relationships.

PRINCIPLE 9: THE ART OF UNITY

You've probably had to break up with someone or cut off friends because all they do is take. Every time they show up, they want something. They don't come to bring something; they come to be a vampire. You're around that person for five minutes, it feels like five hours.

Contribution buys a say-so.

For example, in our church, if someone wants to meet with me (except for crisis counseling or situations) about something that's going on or about how we do something in church? We will check their tithing records. I'll ask our accounting department to check their giving records. We will also check with the ministry coordinator to see if they are serving in the ministry of helps.

See, I want to hear the voices of the people who are serving, who are involved, who are connected and giving to support the organization, because their contribution is what buys them access. And some people want access with no contribution. They just want to talk to you. They want to give their negative input. They seek out something wrong so they can sow division and strife. But to stay unified, I want to hear the voices of people who have skin in the game the same way I do.

I'll give it to you biblically so you don't think I made this up. The Bible describes four types of dirt and only one produced a good harvest. The other three either didn't produce anything, or their seedlings got choked out by the cares of this world, or their lives went upside down because they cared more about stuff than they did about God.

When all hell breaks loose in their life, what will they do? They'll come running back to God.

If an American Express card could save them, they'd get one of those.

If a black car can save you, get one of those. If a Mercedes can save you, get one of those. But God is the only one who can turn a mess around, the only one who can change an entire situation.

And if you didn't know, now you know!

When I contribute to something, then I have more say in it, right? This is why my child does not tell me what's for dinner. You didn't buy it, you ain't making it, you have no say!

"Well, this here is *my* phone." Did you buy that phone? Are you paying the bill for that phone? Because if you are not, that phone belongs to me and it will do what I say it's going to do, whether you like it or not!

My contribution buys my right to voice my opinion. And if my contribution buys my voice, then you have to know that when you bring no contribution, I call the shots on this house. The Bible says, "Endeavor to keep the unity of the Spirit in the bond of peace" (Ephesians 4:3). *Endeavor* means that I contribute, I painstakingly work. In this house, I am the under-shepherd under Jesus., I call the shots in His name. But I can't tell you how many times I have said to somebody who had a different idea, "Let's try that. Let's do that."

I'm telling you, the body of Christ has a spirit of competition. It's a problem.

It's a problem among ministers.

I've been invited places to preach, and I know they're like, "We'll never have him back here again. He's doing too much. My people are going to leave here and go to his church." No, they won't! Wanna know why? Because if they come here, I'm sending them back to you quick, fast, and in a hurry! I've done it!

When people are fearful of your gift, it's because they bring no contribution.

A person who brings a contribution knows what they do well. If my job is to throw the bricks up on the wall, and somebody next to me lays the joint compound, I know that when I throw the brick, if he hasn't laid the joint compound, we have a problem. So contribution buys my unity. I depend on him just like he depends on me.

> **Luke 11:17-20**
> **But he, knowing their thoughts, said unto them, Every kingdom divided against itself is brought to desolation; and a**

PRINCIPLE 9: THE ART OF UNITY

> house divided against a house falleth. If Satan also be divided against himself, how shall his kingdom stand? because ye say that I cast out devils through Beelzebub. And if I by Beelzebub cast out devils, by whom do your sons cast them out? therefore shall they be your judges. But if I with the finger of God cast out devils, no doubt the kingdom of God is come upon you."

Notice how he said with the finger of God? Anytime you hear the hand of God, the finger of God, the arm of God, it refers to the power of God. There is more power in your arm than there is in your hand. There is more power in your hand than there is in your finger—unless you can do the inch punch Bruce Lee used to do, where he could punch you with an inch and throw you across the room.

The arm of God is more powerful than the hand of God. The hand of God is more powerful than the finger of God.

Jesus chose to say, "If I by the *finger* of God"—in other words, in the lowest denomination of power— "…am able to cast out devils, no doubt the Kingdom of God has come upon you."

If you keep going, He helps you understand that no matter how strong you are, one stronger than you can take your armor from you, take all your stuff from you, and divide it up with the ones he's united with.

One of the biggest problems with the body of Christ is thinking you can float the middle.

There is no middle ground.

In real estate, you own up to your property line, right? And if you have a wall or a fence, you own one side of it, and your neighbor owns the other side, even though it's the same brick. So if I want to tear down a wall and put up another one, I've got to talk to my neighbor and say, "Hey, can we unite on this? We'll split the cost and go at this thing together."

If your neighbor won't, then you can't.

People who ride the fence talk about God, but they're never in church. They're never with their church family. They will leave their church in a heartbeat. Big opportunity comes, they leave their church then they wonder why their life is falling apart.

Why can you not ride the fence?

Because Satan owns the fence, there is no neutral ground. You're either going to be part of the solution, or you're part of the problem.

> **Luke 11:24**
> **When the unclean spirit is gone out of a man, he walketh through dry places, seeking rest; and finding none, he saith, I will return unto my house whence I came out.**

You mean to tell me these spirits are talking and thinking?

Let me mess you all up. Let's talk about Lazarus and the rich man.

The leper, Lazarus, died and is in Abraham's bosom. The rich man is also dead. The Bible says he's buried and dead.

He's in hell, and he asks Abraham to go talk to his brothers—which means he remembers his brothers. He remembers his life. Think about this for a second. His body is dead and buried! His brain is dead and buried, but he's still thinking, he's still feeling, he's feeling love for his brothers. He's emotional, he's talking about where he wants them to go. He can feel pain.

He's like, "Could you just put a drop of water on my tongue here?"

So in Luke 11, Jesus is describing these spirits walking through dry places, seeking rest and finding none.

It's interesting that when God gets people delivered from some things, some of them have the audacity to then leave God. God cleans them up, repaints the inside, puts down some hardwood floors, puts marble and granite on the countertops. He makes it all beautiful, and then they've got the nerve to go back to the world. So when the spirits come back to them, they find a house swept clean, and they realize that person didn't fill it with God things.

PRINCIPLE 9: THE ART OF UNITY

See, they were supposed to fill up that house so that there was no room for demonic entities to come back. But they weren't paying attention because they were chasing the money, chasing the stuff, chasing things. They didn't care about their spiritual state! They thought it wasn't important to go to church. They thought it wasn't important to feed their spirit. So now Satan comes back and finds a swept and garnished house.

Are demons smarter than you? Remember what Jesus said? He said the children of the world are smarter than children of light, because even the children of the world know how to work the world system. So they're smarter than the children of light. Because children of light don't know how to work the light system. He wasn't commending the unjust steward's behavior; He was saying "at least this dude in his unjustness had enough sense to understand the system he worked in and to work that thing."

If a spirit who's stronger than you comes in and takes over your house, you've got to go.

So the spirits are smarter and have more wisdom than you, because the spirit says, "I come back, the house is empty. But I got overtaken the first time, so let me go get some of my people stronger than me to partner and unite with so I can come back stronger."

Back in the day, a king would have a harem, which is a bunch of women. They were all his wives. I have no idea why any man would want more than one wife—that's like trying to drive two cars at the same time.

But here's what they did: They made eunuchs out of the men who guarded and tended to the women. In other words, they castrated them. Think about this for a second. The reason why the kings castrated the men who tended to the women was so that the men who tended to the women couldn't do anything *with* the women, right? Because a castrated man has no parts.

Why do demons have the ability to find somebody stronger, but Christians want to castrate one another and reduce their abilities?

"I feel better when you're around because you're lesser than me. You can't pray like me. You don't have an anointing like me. You make me feel better because you are lesser than me."

We Christians run around making eunuchs while demons are strategizing: "Wait a minute, you've got a greater strength than I do. Come with me. I don't care if I sleep in the master bedroom or in a spare bedroom. I don't care if I sleep on the couch. I just want you to bring your gifts into the house because I know that when someone stronger than me comes, I've got some backup that can say 'hold on, you're not coming this far, stop it right now!'"

The reason you can't get the victory is you surround yourself with people who are less than you. You better round up some folks who'll bring you up and cause you to come up in lights!

The Bible says that whenever power and unity were present, the believers were in one accord. And when they were in one accord, the clouds rolled in, the power stepped in, and cloven tongues of fire sat on their heads! The power of God will roll into the house because people have got the same mind, the same purpose. They want the same things. They're not complaining about what kind of toilet paper the church uses. They're not complaining about what the floor looks like. They're not complaining about what type of seat they sit in. They're not complaining about stuff that does not matter. They are unified — one front.

Learn how to bring a supply as you participate in the Body.

It never fails—there are always people who just come to take. People will ask about our benevolence fund. And when I say it's for people in our church, they're like "Why is that? Can't you make an exception?" No, because when I tell you "yes," then I'll have to say "no" to someone who's in our church and makes a contribution.

> **John 17:11**
> **And now I am no more in the world, but these are in the world, and I come to thee. Holy Father, keep through thine own name those whom thou hast given me, that they may be one, as we are.**

PRINCIPLE 9: THE ART OF UNITY

The reason why some people never seem to go up is that they're not unified.

"You know what? It's all about us coming into the unity of faith, so whatever you want me to do, I'll do however you want me to do it. I just want to be in the game. I don't have an opinion; I don't have a way to do it; I'll do whatever. It's fine!"

When you have unity, you have power. People need to jettison their feelings, their emotions, and their thoughts, and say, "You know what? What do we have to do and how can we do it together?" Now my gift blesses her. My gift blesses him.

When it's God, whatever she takes from his gift doesn't shortchange him, because God can bless both at the same time. Because he's God!

And if I'm anointed, I can come home and be a husband and a father to my kids. I can preach the paint off the walls, run my businesses, do all the things I'm supposed to do, and still keep my joy and my peace, still function in unity, still discern my part to play, and still bring my supply.

I don't have to be like, "Well, I can't come to church today because I've gotta go to work." I know where my supply really comes from. I'm coming here, and if you're going to fire me, deuces!

I'll stay with God because I know where my help comes from, and I'm going to stay unified with this people.

I've been trying to get our leadership to understand some things since we started the church 10 years ago. Some parts of it are still unclear to them, but I'm patient. Why?

Because I can't do it by myself. If I could take it out of my head and put it in theirs like a USB download, I would have! But it's taken me 10 years.

That's the mission. That's understanding that if we *all* ain't going, I ain't going.

When my pastor was at church, I never left until he left, because I was serving closely with him. If he didn't leave, I didn't leave. If we were working on a project, I didn't leave until we were all done. *Unity.*

Why? Because the moment I left, it was going to take longer. So I brought my supply so we could hurry this thing up. Nowadays, if I've got something to do after church, then I'm going to help you all get your stuff done so we can *all* go home. This is what unity looks like.

They were all in one accord—thinking the same thing, believing the same thing, breathing the same air, wanting the same things, chasing after the same thing. They all had one accord and when that happened, the power of God descended into the building. The whole building shook with the power of God. Why? Because God is attracted to unity, and not strife.

If you've got something against somebody in the church, get over it. Go and apologize. Say, "I am so sorry that I have not liked you for all this time. Did I ever tell you how pretty your eyes are?"

We cannot afford that nonsense. Some of you are upset with people and you've been holding on to that junk that they did to you when you were like, two, and now you're 50-something years old and *still* holding on to that nonsense. You need to let go and move on.

You need to be unified in this thing, or else you'll keep fighting over nonsense. You'll keep having strife and division over *nonsense*, and you will hold the rest of us off from going into the Promised Land! We'll all be sitting there looking at these big old fat grapes, saying, "Boy, these sure look good!"

I don't know about you, but I love me some cotton candy grapes. They're hard to find, but when I do find them? I'll share everything with my child *but* my cotton candy grapes.

My wife asks me to make my child's plate and I'm like, "Whoa, whoa, whoa! Let me just put on a couple, cut 'em in quarters so it looks like more." Pastor ain't completely saved yet. I'm working on it!

PRINCIPLE 9: THE ART OF UNITY

Listen, we have got to understand the power of unity. We've got to understand the power of coming together and forsaking our own selves—not submitting because you think someone is stronger, but because you think more highly of them than you do of yourself.

Don't run around with your feelings on your sleeve, just looking for a reason to get out of church.

"Pastor said boo-boo! See, I told you, I'm out of here!" Really? That's why you're leaving?

Just looking for a reason!

We used to say in sales, "If you want to get off a sales call with a person, just hang up the phone. Don't try to talk them out of a sale, just hang up on them! Better yet, don't even make the call—just quit." The entire purpose of a sales call is to sell, not to un-sell.

So if you don't want to go to church then don't. Quit looking for a reason to not go, to substantiate your bias and disobedience. Unity is everything. And Satan knows that as long as he and his minions can keep you divided against the institution Jesus established for your protection, then you will never go to church. And, unfortunately, never grow into all that God has for you.

As long as he can keep a husband divided against his wife, y'all will never come into the fullness of what is meant for your home. As long as he can keep everybody nitpicking, critical, and fighting—"Well, I think we should do it this way! No, we *definitely* should do it that way!" Let's pick one and then we'll all just do that for the sake of unity.

"I'll be nice to them if they apologize to me!" How about *you* just go apologize to *them*?

And don't be one of those people who are like, "I didn't do anything wrong, but I'm apologizing to you anyway!" And then sit back and hope that they say they're sorry too. And then when they don't, you walk away.

Why don't you be the bigger person?

www.ingramcontent.com/pod-product-compliance
Lightning Source LLC
LaVergne TN
LVHW052254070426
835507LV00035B/2891